THE BATTLE IN THE BAYOU COUNTRY

THE BATTLE IN THE BAYOU COUNTRY

By Morris Raphael

Illustrations on jacket, title page, and beginning of chapters
By Chestee Harrington Minvielle

HARLO DETROIT

First Edition

1404 Bayou Side Drive
New Iberia, Louisiana 70560

Printed by Harlo Press, 16721 Hamilton Avenue, Detroit, Michigan 48203

DEDICATED

TO

MY WIFE HELEN

ACKNOWLEDGMENTS

Without my wife's help this book would have been impossible. *Helen* didn't nag me about the multitude of chores which were left undone and kept the kids quiet, occupied and happy. Furthermore her assistance in the way of proofreading and good judgment were essential contributions. Thanks to my daughter, *Rose Anne,* and my son, *John,* for their valuable aid—especially in compiling the index.

A friend who played a tremendous part in the production of this book was *Miss Barbara Kyle* of New Iberia. Her hard work in typing and retyping the manuscript, her constructive comments and words of encouragement were indeed appreciated. We would have been lost without her constant help—which she so graciously volunteered.

Our thanks go out to Barbara's sister, *Virginia Kyle Hine,* who first got us interested in the Bayou Country conflict. A dozen years ago *Virginia* posed us with the problem of helping her locate Camp Pratt. Recently, we found the exact location of the camp. But better yet, during our extensive research we garnered enough information to write a book.

We were very fortunate in acquiring the help of *Chestee Harrington Minvielle* who is heralded as one of the top artists in the State of Louisiana. *Chestee's* illustrations alone make this book a collector's item.

I owe a debt of gratitude to my good friend, *Robert Angers, Jr.* of Lafayette, for getting me back on the writing trail. In my opinion *Bob* is one of the leading journalists in the South and I've learned a lot from the ole master.

Thanks to *Professor David Edmonds,* of the University of Southwestern Louisiana, Lafayette, for assisting me in my research. *Dr. Edmonds* is writing a sequel to this book. The cooperation of *Dennis Gibson* and *Glenn Conrad* of USL was also helpful and appreciated.

Others who assisted and encouraged this writer were *Dr. Tom Kramer,* former State Senator *Wilbur Kramer,* the late *Pres Gates* and the *Tom Holmes* of Franklin; *George Ernest, Jimmy Schwing, Mrs. Thomas Disch,* and Parish Assessor *Clegg Labauve* of New Iberia; *Dr. Richard Saloom* of Lafayette; *Bill Moore* of Baton Rouge; *Walter Landry* of Jeanerette; the librarians of Iberia, St. Martin and St. Mary parishes; *Professor Cecil Eby* of the University of Michigan; *Dr. Ed Sloan* and *Mrs. Marian Clarke* of Trinity College, Hartford, Connecticut; and there were many, many more.

My heartfelt thanks go out to all of these fine people.

CONTENTS

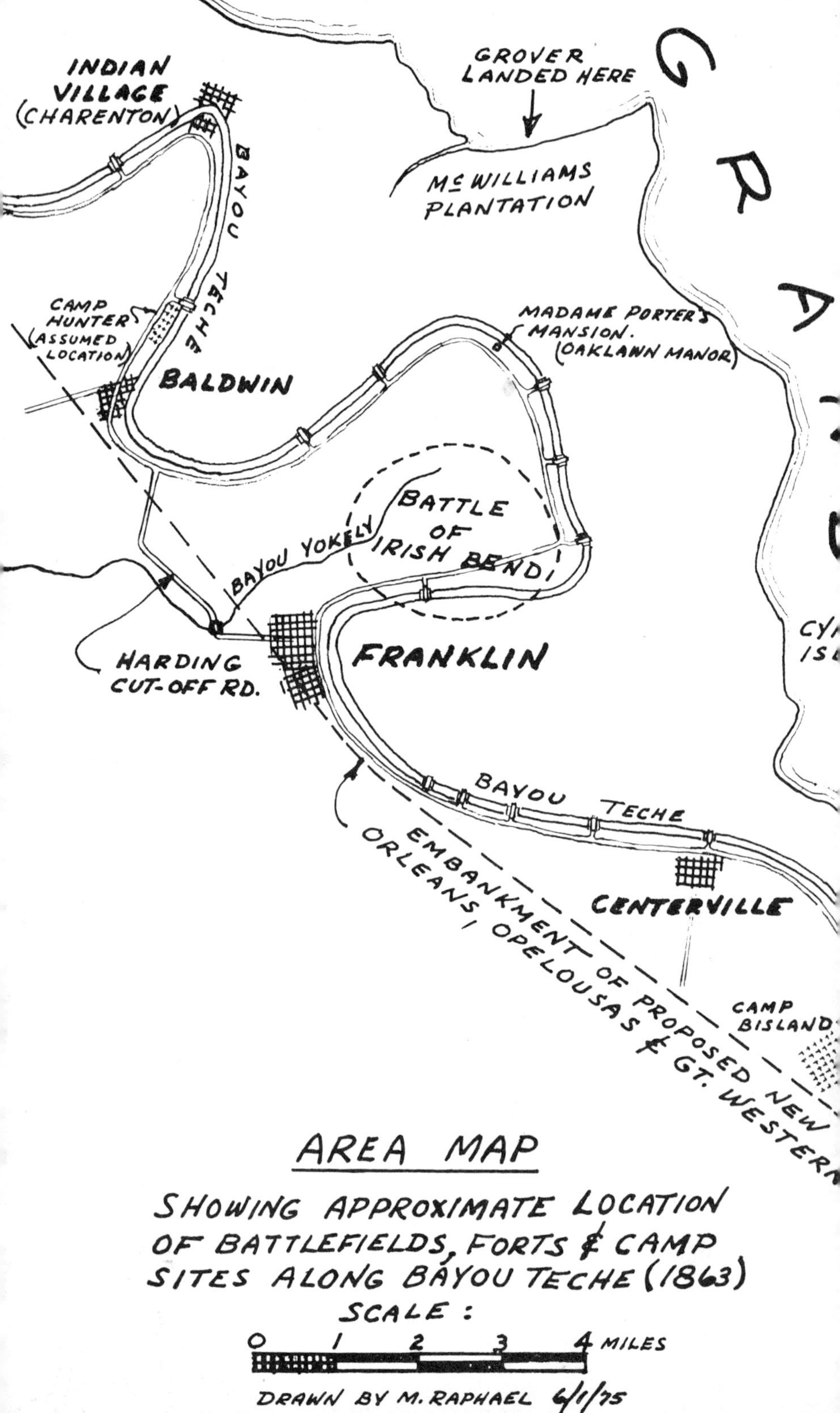
INDIAN VILLAGE (CHARENTON)
GROVER LANDED HERE
McWILLIAMS PLANTATION
BAYOU TECHE
CAMP HUNTER (ASSUMED LOCATION)
BALDWIN
MADAME PORTER'S MANSION. (OAKLAWN MANOR)
BATTLE OF IRISH BEND
BAYOU YOKELY
HARDING CUT-OFF RD.
FRANKLIN
BAYOU TECHE
CENTERVILLE
CAMP BISLAND
EMBANKMENT OF PROPOSED NEW ORLEANS, OPELOUSAS & GT. WESTERN
AREA MAP
SHOWING APPROXIMATE LOCATION OF BATTLEFIELDS, FORTS & CAMP SITES ALONG BAYOU TECHE (1863)
SCALE:
0 1 2 3 4 MILES
DRAWN BY M. RAPHAEL 6/1/75

N
AKE
FLAT
LAKE
BAYOU TECHE
ATCHAFALAYA B.
TTLE
OF
LAND
PATTERSONVILLE
ATCHAFALAYA RIVER
BERWICK
BERWICK BAY
FORT
BUCHANA
BRASHEA
CITY
ATCHAFALAYA RIVER
BAYOU SHAFFER

FOREWORD

This book is meant to be entertaining as well as factual. Some war histories tend to bore the reader with technical details and overstatement of insignificant action. The author has made a sincere effort to maintain interest by sticking to the basic facts and injecting human interest as the story progresses. During research we found that the contemporary war scribe minimized his own casualties, compounded those of the enemy and brought out atrocities that made the opponents look like villains. Assurance is given here that the author has researched his subject thoroughly and attempts to be as authentic and impartial as possible.

We also learned that most battle scribes occasionally turned their backs to the rigors of war and took time out to describe the natural beauty of this bayou wonderland.

Confederate General Richard Taylor gave this flowery account in his immortal work entitled *Destruction and Reconstruction:*

> "A few miles above the railway terminus at Berwick's (Bay) there enters from the west the Teche, loveliest of southern streams. Navigable for more than

a hundred miles, preserving at all seasons an equal breadth and depth, so gentle is its flow that it might be taken for a canal, did not the charming and graceful curves, by which it separates the undulating prairies of Attakapas from the alluvion of the Atchafalaya, mark it as the handiwork of nature.

"Before the war, the Teche for fifty miles, from Berwick's Bay to New Iberia, passed through one field of sugar canes, the fertile and well-cultivated estates succeeding each other. The mansions of the opulent planters, as well as the villages of their slaves, were situated on the west bank of the bayou overlooking the broad, verdant prairie, where countless herds roamed. On the east bank, the dense forest had given way to fields of luxuriant canes; and to connect the two parts of estates, floating bridges were constructed, with openings in the center for the passage of steamers.

"Stately live oaks, the growth of centuries, orange groves, and flowers of every hue and fragrance, surrounded the abodes of the 'seigneurs'; while within, one found the grace of the 'salon' combined with the healthy cheeriness of country life. Abundance and variety of game encouraged field sports, and the waters, fresh and salt, swarmed with fish. With the sky and temperature of Sicily, the breezes from prairie and Gulf were as health-giving as those that ripple the heather on Scotch moors.

"In all my wanderings, and they have been many and wide, I can not recall so fair, so bountiful, and so happy a land."[1]

James K. Hosmer of the 52nd Regiment of the Massachusetts Volunteers wrote a chapter in his book *The Color Guard* relating to a march that was made from Donaldsonville to Thibodaux along Bayou Lafourche. He described this beautiful stretch as the "Garden of Louisiana." The following are excerpts from this chapter.

"Seldom does an army march under circumstances so delightful. The miles were not dreary ones; for the same

> really remarkable conditions made our progress comparatively easy from first to last,—a bright sky and sun, but a cool northern breeze, and a road, for the most part, in perfect condition to receive the soldier's footfall.
>
> "Plantation after plantation! Along the road were white palings, or often the pleasanter enclosure of a rose-tree hedge, with white roses all out, and a green of a richer depth than we know it. Then, between house and hedge, those marvelous gardens! Tall trees overhung them; with vines, sometimes nearly as thick as the trunks, twining, supple as serpents, from root to the topmost bough,—twining, hanging in loops, knotted in coils. Then, underneath, flowers white and delicate, adorned with dewy jewels, scented with odors incomparable.
>
> "Such tropic luxury of air and vegetation! These scents and zephyrs; the bird-songs we heard; the summer-blue of the heavens; the broad palm-trees at the planter's portico; these blossoms of crimson and saffron and white. The air would be pungent with sweetness as the column marched past."[2]

Another vivid description of the bayou country beauty was given by Lt. Henry Hill Goodell, 25th Connecticut Volunteers, aboard a stern-wheel steamer from Barry's Landing (Port Barre) along the Bayou Cortableau and down the Atchafalaya River to Brashear City (Morgan City). Here is some of what he wrote:

> "Never shall I forget the beauty of that sail. We were dropping down one of those little bayous that intersect the state in every direction. The spring freshets had swollen the stream and set its waters far back into the forests that lined its banks on either side. Festoons of Spanish moss, drooped like a mourning veil from bough to bough. Running vines with bright colored sprays of flowers twined in and out among the branches of the trees. The purple passion flowers flung its (sic) starry blossoms to the world, the sign and symbol of the suf-

> fering Savior. While the yellow jasmine, crested herons, snowy white, roses from the water, and stretching their long necks and legs out into a straight line with their bodies, winged their flight above the tree-tops. Pelicans displayed their ungainly forms, as they snapped at the passing fish and neatly laid them away for future reference in their pouches. Strange birds of gaudy plummage flew from side to side, harshly screaming as they hid themselves in the dense foliage. Huge alligators sunned themselves along the shore, or showed their savage muzzles, as they slowly swam across our path."[3]

Yet there were some accounts which were not so flowery or filled with praise about the wonders of nature. One such report was that recorded by Captain John De Forest of the 12th Connecticut Volunteers, in his book *A Volunteer's Adventure,* describing his frustrations at Camp Parapet near New Orleans.

> He wrote, "Sitting in my tent, with the sides looped all around, I am drenched with perspiration. I come in from inspection (which means standing half an hour in the sun) with coat and trousers almost dripping wet, and my soaked sash stained with the blue of my uniform. There is no letup, no relenting, to the heat. Morning after morning the same brazen sun inflames the air till we go about with mouths open like suffering dogs. Toward noon clouds appear, gusts of wind struggle to overset our tents, and sheets of rain turn the camp into a marsh, but bring no permanent coolness.
>
> "The night air is as heavy and dank as that of a swamp, and at daybreak the rotten odor of the earth is sickening. It is a land moreover of vermin, at least in this season. The tent hums with them like a beehive, audible rods away; as Lieutenant Potter says, they sing like canary birds. When I slip under my mosquito bar they prowl and yell around me with the ferocity of panthers.
>
> "Tiny millers and soft green insects get in my eyes, stick to my perspiring face, and perish by scores in the

> flame of my candle. Various kinds of brilliant bugs drop on my paper, where they are slain and devoured by gangs of large red ants. These ants rummage my whole habitation for rations, crawl into my clothing and under my blanket at night, and try to eat me alive."[4]

It is important to mention here that among the inhabitants of the bayou country were many of the descendants of the Acadians who were exiled from Canada in the 1750's and settled in South Louisiana. Records reveal that these people fought valiantly for the Confederate cause not only in Louisiana but across the nation as well.

Great prominence has been placed upon battles that were fought in New Orleans, Baton Rouge, Port Hudson, Mansfield and other Louisiana areas, but very little has been written about the action in the bayou country. The average person does not realize that thousands upon thousands of casualties were suffered by brave men from both sides in this particular arena of warfare.

It is therefore this writer's intention to publicize in this one volume a great many historical events and interesting situations that have been overshadowed by the big battles and were overlooked by the contemporary journalists.

CHAPTER I

FROM THE BEGINNING

The War Between the States was declared on April 12, 1861, and patriots in the bayou country lost no time in answering the call to arms. Shortly thereafter, a steady stream of Confederate volunteers began embarking for military training camps in the New Orleans area, and also to Camp Moore, north of Amite.[1]

In nearly every town a glorious send-off was enacted. There were parades, bands, fireworks, speeches, shouting, singing, hugging, kissing, weeping and praying. At New Iberia a boat-load of volunteers left from the steamboat dock at the foot of Serrett Street after receiving the accolades of a noisy delegation.[2] In Franklin, Miss Louise McKerall, a beautiful young lady, delivered a stirring speech to the newly formed St. Mary Cannoneers. As she presented the group with a flag, she uttered these historic words, "Return with it, and may its folds forever shield you."[3]

The New Orleans, Opelousas and Great Western Railroad, which at that time extended from Brashear to Algiers, was giving free passage to recruits. Brashear City (now known as Morgan City) was the railroad terminus for the Berwick Bay area. This area included Berwick and Pattersonville (now known as Patterson).[4]

In St. Landry Parish, troops were organized at Camp Overton near Opelousas and departed by steamboat from Washington. The local steamboat companies were not to be outdone by the generosity of the railroads, so they also donated trips to the enlistees. A steamboat could carry an amazing number of men aboard. The *Opelousas Courier* reported on March 15,1862, that 1000 men from six different cavalry companies were jam-packed aboard the steamer *Nina Semmes.*

Boats from this particular area generally moved from Washington along Bayou Courtableau to Bayou Plaquemine and then to the Mississippi down to New Orleans. Here the troops were assembled at Camp Roman, formed into regiments and dispatched to the battle fronts.[5]

Some troops, however marched the entire distance to the training camps, picking up men along the way. One such example was the Eighteenth Louisiana Regiment commanded by Colonel Alfred Mouton of Vermilionville (Lafayette) who has been revered as the champion of the Acadians. The handsome West Pointer, while leading his troops astride his beautiful stallion "Attakapas," was joined by volunteers from the parishes of Lafayette, St. Landry, St. Martin, Vermilion, St. Mary, St. James and Orleans. It was reported that troops from as far away as Natchitoches and Calcasieu parishes made their way across the state to join the column.[6]

Because of the Union blockade of the Gulf Coast in 1861, coastal passenger service was suspended and inland transportation in South Louisiana became a necessity. One such system, called the "Texas, New Orleans and Great Western Passenger Route," promised Houston to New Orleans service in 70 hours. The passengers were transported between Houston and Niblett's Bluff (Vinton) by rail. From this point they experienced a rough overland trip to New Iberia by stagecoach, then New Iberia to Berwick's

Bay by river packets. The remainder of the route, Brashear to New Orleans, was by rail.[7]

Patriotism ran high in the beginning and it was reported during November, 1861, that there were 23,577 troops from Louisiana who were serving under the Confederate flag. This represented the largest number from any Southern state based on population, except for the state of Virginia.[8]

But five months later, volunteering had declined to the point whereby the conscription of troops became necessary. On April 16, 1862, the Confederate congress passed the Conscription Act which declared that every able-bodied white man between the ages of eighteen and thirty-five became subject to military service for a period of three years.[9]

Since police juries in southern Louisiana were dominated by top sugarmen, who anticipated the disruption of their slave labor on the plantations, there was apparently no problem in voting funds for military purposes. In some cases the jurors even saw fit to appropriate money for the support of families of volunteers. Judge William T. Palfrey, well-known sugar planter from St. Mary Parish, delivered a sparkling address during a patriotic meeting in Franklin on April 23, He was one of many orators from the area who appeared on the platform in competition to secure enlistment and money for the Confederate cause. Their efforts proved to be a great success and furthermore paved the way for the police jury to appropriate $20,000 for defense of the parish and state.[10]

Bayou country women also did their part in promoting the Confederate cause. They put on bazaars, suppers, dances, shows and other types of entertainment to raise money. The ladies even made uniforms for the soldiers. It was noted that each parish had its own style and color of uniform with red, blue and brown predominating.[11]

But as the months rolled by, state officials and citizens found themselves in a pathetic situation. Nearly all Louisiana troops were fighting on fronts outside the state, and money, arms and ammunition were being drained for the support of other areas. But, worse yet, the enemy had ap-

UNION GENERAL BENJAMIN BUTLER

peared on the state scene and was now planning to capture the South's largest city—New Orleans.[12]

Union Major General Benjamin Butler was assigned to the project and placed in command of the Department of the Gulf. On March 20th he arrived at Ship Island, which is located off the Mississippi Gulf Coast, and in a short period of time collected a ground force of around 13,500 troops.[13] Confederate Major General Mansfield Lovell was in command of the land units which protected the vast New Orleans area but his forces only numbered around 5,000.

U. S. Flag Officer David Farragut was in command of the West Gulf Squadron and also the naval portion of the expedition which was destined for the reduction of New Orleans.

But that was not an easy task as there were two mighty fortresses which protected the Crescent City. They were Forts Jackson and St. Philip located across the river from each other at a point some seventy-five miles below New Orleans.[14] Nevertheless, Farragut's gunboat armada assisted by Commander David Porter's mortar flotilla were poised downstream of the forts waiting the proper time to attack.

The bombardment of Fort Jackson began on April 16th[15] and about 3:30 a.m. of the 24th "all hell broke loose" as Farragut with 17 gunboats decided to run the gauntlet of the two forts. In spite of the excessive and unrelenting hail of gunfire from the fortresses, concealed land batteries and gunboats, he succeeded in his daring venture. He reported his losses as minimal and that eleven of the enemies' steamer gunboats, which protected the forts, were either destroyed or captured.[16]

In the meantime Butler's superior land forces smashed whatever resistance they encountered and succeeded in capturing the strategic points along the river. Butler entered New Orleans on May 1, 1862, and began what was heralded as the most notorious military occupation of the War Between the States.[17]

Sugar was the chief industry in southern Louisiana and at the outbreak of the war there were 1,291 sugar plantations operating with approximately 139,000 slaves. With

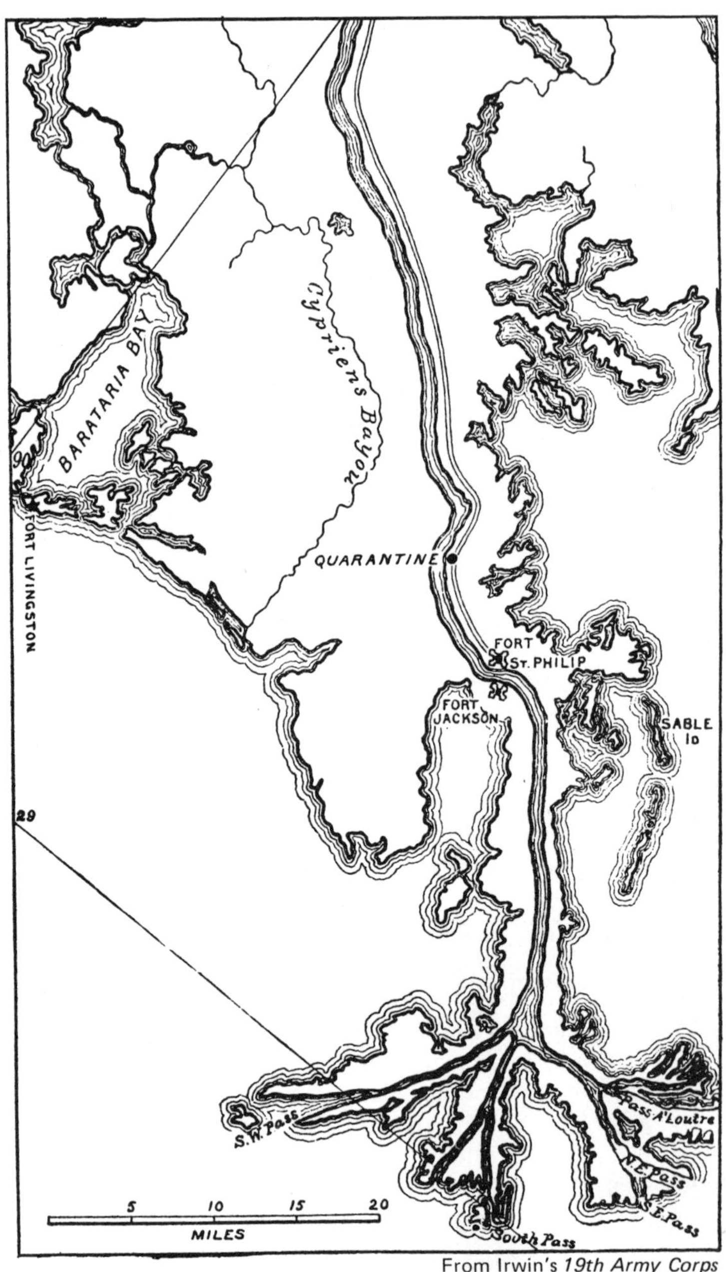

From Irwin's *19th Army Corps*

FORTS AT LOWER END OF MISSISSIPPI RIVER

the Yankee takeover of New Orleans, the planters felt that their great investments in sugar and slaves were in jeopardy. They knew General "Beast" Butler's reputation, and were concerned that he would not only destroy the economy of the area, but would reign as a pompous conqueror as well.[18]

The glamour and enthusiasm that existed when war began had now been transformed into a sort of terror. Military reverses had lowered the morale of the people and they began clamoring to Governor Thomas O. Moore for protection.

Following the fall of New Orleans, Gov. Moore moved the state capitol from Baton Rouge to Opelousas. He set up the state capitol in the home of his friend, Alexander Mouton, on the corner of Grolee and Liberty streets.[19] He then wrote President Jefferson Davis that the Confederate forces in Louisiana were disorganized and that this situation was causing unrest and internal dissension.[20]

The Federal occupation of Baton Rouge on May 28th added to the miseries of Gov. Moore. The Confederacy then formed a new department called the Trans-Mississippi which included the State of Louisiana, but the governor felt that very little help could be obtained here. So he began the organization of troops for the defense of the state and built training camps at Opelousas, Monroe and New Iberia.[21]

Prior to mid-1862, there was very little action in the bayou country and very few Confederate troops. It appeared that most of the fighting in Louisiana had taken place along the Mississippi River. New Orleans and Baton Rouge, which had fallen to the Federal forces, had received the brunt of the battle thus far and now Port Hudson was under seige.

Another river town, Donaldsonville, was dealt a disastrous blow as the result of unfortunate circumstances. It so happened that a group of Texas Partisan Rangers under command of Captain James A. McWaters had embarked upon the dangerous sport of firing upon Federal transports and other vessels which passed along the river. On July 22,

1862, the Federals threatened to shell the town if the sniper action continued.[22]

Four days later the Mayor of Donaldsonville, on behalf of the citizens, pleaded with McWaters to stop firing. McWaters replied that he would stop for the time being, but would have to confer with Gov. Moore. The Governor called a conference in Thibodaux on July 31st and undoubtedly overruled the mayor's objections, because McWaters returned to continue firing away at the enemy vessels.[23]

Farragut became enraged and ordered the evacuation of men, women and children from Donaldsonville, declaring the town would be bombarded within three days. The population, of course, departed, and on the morning of August 9th Farragut stuck to his threat and sent several of his gunboats, which shelled the city for several hours. Afterwards a detachment was sent ashore with torches and before long this river settlement was ablaze. The destruction included most of the business section of the town, a number of houses and some plantations along the river.

Farragut left the people of Donaldsonville this grim message: "Every time my boats are fired upon, I will burn a portion of your town."[24]

St. Vincent's Catholic Institute had sustained damages as the result of the raid and a protest was filed by the Sisters of Charity. Evidently Butler felt that the incident had placed his own moral standing in jeopardy. So he immediately submitted a long letter of apology to Sister Clara, supervisor of the school.

He wrote that he was "very, very sorry" that the Sister's establishment had been destroyed as a result of the shelling and maintained that the injury was accidental. Butler declared that the inhabitants of Donaldsonville harbored "a gang of cowardly guerrillas who committed every atrocity." He maintained that these guerrillas fired upon an unarmed boat, crowded with women—many of whom had been in school in New Orleans.[25]

As an act of restitution Butler offered to fill the Sister's order for provisions and medicine and assured them of continued respect and help from his officers and men.

But Butler was a hated man. Because of his reported uncouth and inhumane actions, he was labeled as "The Beast" by the citizens of the Confederacy. He could have written a thousand letters of apology to cover the atrocities committed by him and his men, but the people knew him for what he was worth.

They remembered how William B. Mumford, a citizen of New Orleans, was cruelly executed for pulling down a U.S. flag before the city had formally surrendered. They also remembered the infamous "General Order No. 28" issued May 15, 1862, that read in part:[26]

> "Hereafter when any female shall by word, gesture, or movement insult or show contempt for any officer or soldier of the United States she shall be regarded and held liable to be treated as a woman of the town plying her avocation."

There were charges that peaceful and aged citizens were confined at hard labor with ball and chain and that helpless women were torn from their homes and subjected to solitary confinement. Also it was reported that sugar planters were threatened with having slaves driven from the plantations unless the owners consented to share the crops with General Butler, his brother Andrew J. Butler and other Union officers.[27]

There were accusations that the entire population of New Orleans was forced to choose between starvation by the confiscation of all their property or taking an oath against conscience to bear allegiance to the invaders of the country. There were reports that slaves had been incited to insurrection and armed for a servile war—"a war in its nature far exceeding in horrors the most merciless atrocities of the savages."[28]

Butler even received criticism from his own officers. Lt. F. A. Roe, commander of the U.S. Gunboat *Katahdin,* while escorting three transports to Donaldsonville on September 11th, stated in a report to Commodore Henry Mor-

From Library of Congress

CONFEDERATE GENERAL RICHARD TAYLOR

ris that the activities of Federal troops were both "disgraceful and humiliating."

He reported that troops had entered a large mansion, pillaged it in a brutal manner and carried off wines, liquors, silver and clothing belonging to the women. He added that the soldiers were intoxicated, undisciplined and licentious. Lt. Roe asked to be relieved of service requiring him to guard troops engaged in such disgraceful acts.[29]

CHAPTER II

GENERAL TAYLOR ARRIVES

On July 28, 1862, Richard Taylor was detached from the Second Louisiana Brigade, promoted to the rank of major general and assigned to command the Confederate forces in the District of Western Louisiana.[1] It may be well to mention here that General Taylor was prominent in many respects. He was the son of President Zachary Taylor, the brother-in-law of Confederate President Jeff Davis, a member of the Louisiana Legislature, the owner of a sugar plantation in St. Charles Parish, and a hero in the Virginia campaign.

Taylor was well informed in the art of battle having received "on the scene" coaching from the master himself, his father, during the Mexican campaign. Dick Taylor's experience in the Virginia arena of warfare, coupled with his knowledge of Louisiana swamps, made him an ideal choice for the new post.

However, due to a siege of paralysis in his lower limbs, he was compelled to remain in Richmond for several weeks. Having completely recovered, he spent a few days in Chattanooga, Tennessee with his friend General Braxton Bragg

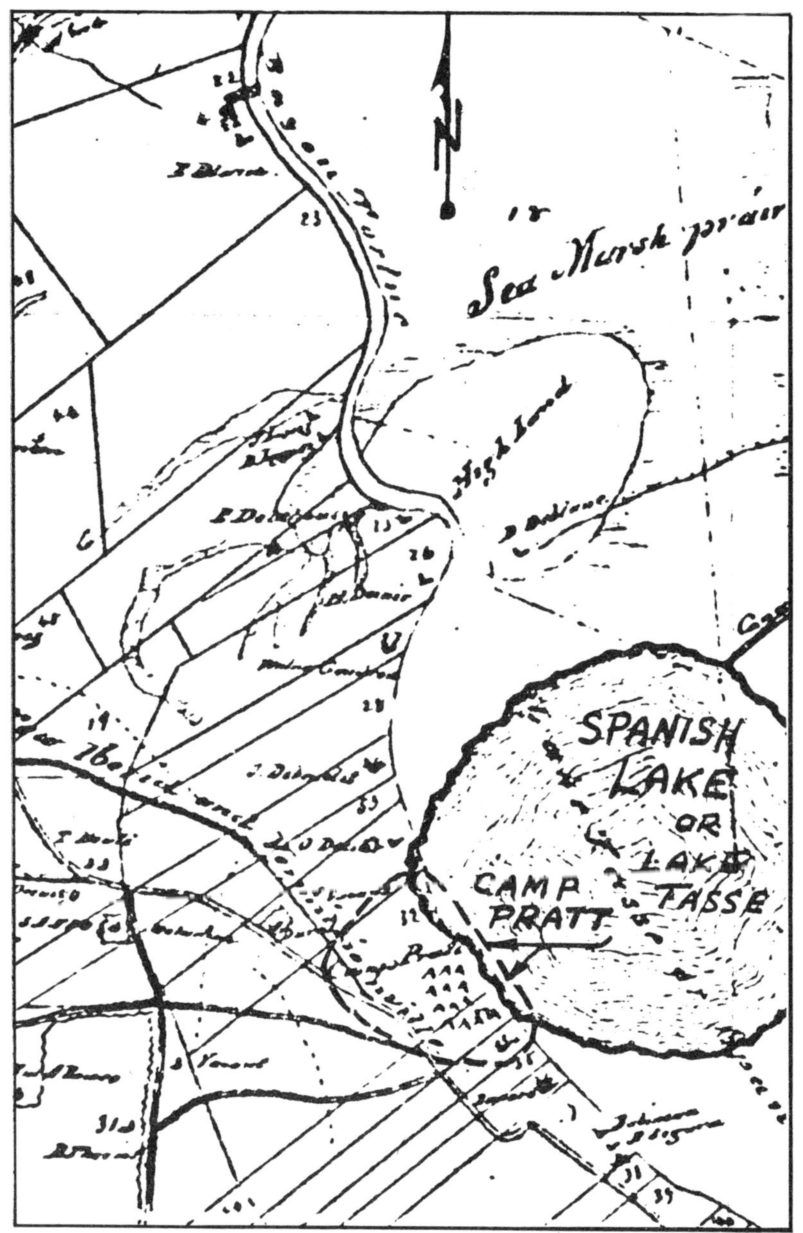

CAMP PRATT – 6 MILES NORTHWEST OF NEW IBERIA
A BLOW-UP OF AN OLD MAP

who had fought under Zack Taylor. Then he headed for western Louisiana. He navigated the Red River and after entering the Atchafalaya he was fortunate in finding a steamer which took him to Bayou Courtableau. However, the Courtableau was too low for steamer navigation and Taylor hired a boat with four Negro oarsmen to make the 20 mile trip up the bayou. He wrote "the narrow stream was over-arched by trees shrouded with Spanish moss, the unusual parasite of southern forests. Heavy rainfall, accompanied by vivid lightning, the flashes of which enabled us to find our way; and before dawn I had the happiness to embrace my wife and children after a separation of fourteen months." Taylor's family had been staying with friends near Washington. Gov. Moore brought them in from St. Charles Parish at the time Farragut's fleet was approaching.[2]

Taylor then met with Gov. Moore in Opelousas and was briefed on the sad situation he had inherited in the way of men and supplies. Gov. Moore turned the small bodies of troops and camp sites he had halfway organized over to Taylor and the general immediately took charge, making Alexandria the headquarters of his district.

Taylor indicated that he had found one camp of instruction established at Monroe but was disappointed that few conscripts had enrolled there. He then established a camp of instruction at Camp Pratt which was located on Lake Tasse near the Nickerson Pecan Grove and about six miles northwest of New Iberia. This camp was named after John G. Pratt of the Parish of Saint Landry who was a brigadier general in the state militia.[3]

Taylor placed Lt. Colonel Burke of the Second Louisiana Regiment in command at Camp Pratt and before long succeeded in enrolling about 3,000 persons as conscripts. Of this number nearly 2,000 were ordered to his district and the remainder sent to Louisiana troops serving at or near Port Hudson. Later Lt. Colonel Burke was replaced by Colonel Eugene Waggaman and returned to his regiment in Virginia.[4]

Major J. L. Brent, who was assigned to the Teche area

as Taylor's chief of ordnance and artillery, lost no time in getting acquainted with his new job. Batteries were equipped, disciplined and drilled; leather was tanned, harness made and wagons built. A little workshop in New Iberia, which was established by Governor Moore, was developed into an important arsenal of construction.[5]

There was a critical need for paper as it was used in the making of cartridges. The paper shortage became so severe that most newspapers in the bayou country were forced to discontinue their operations. While searching for the material, Brent found that a newspaper in Franklin was still in operation. The journal there was being published on wallpaper. Brent then succeeded in finding a quantity of wall paper in the shops in the New Iberia—Franklin area.[6]

Taylor was satisfied with his energetic new assistant and stated that he was impressed with Brent's ability and accomplishments.

There had been no Confederate victories in the State of Louisiana since about the time of the fall of New Orleans and the morale of the people had now reached a new low. The Federals were reportedly plundering homes, smashing furniture and looting precious articles. Much of this was being done in the area of St. Charles Parish including Taylor's home and plantation.[7]

Colonel Edwin Waller, Jr. and his cavalry of Texas riflemen had reported to Taylor around the first of August. This battalion along with General Pratt's state militia units were ordered to attack the Federal outpost at Bayou Des Allemands.

The invading Confederate force played havoc at Des Allemands and Boutte, capturing two companies of infantry including guns and ammunition, burning a railroad station and setting fire to transports and bridges. Louisiana rejoiced at this victory, small though it was.[8]

General Butler's report on September 11, 1862, stated that Waller, by an abuse of a flag of truce, caused the surrender of those troops stationed at Bayou Des Allemands. He wrote "the guerrillas (Confederates) then proceeded to

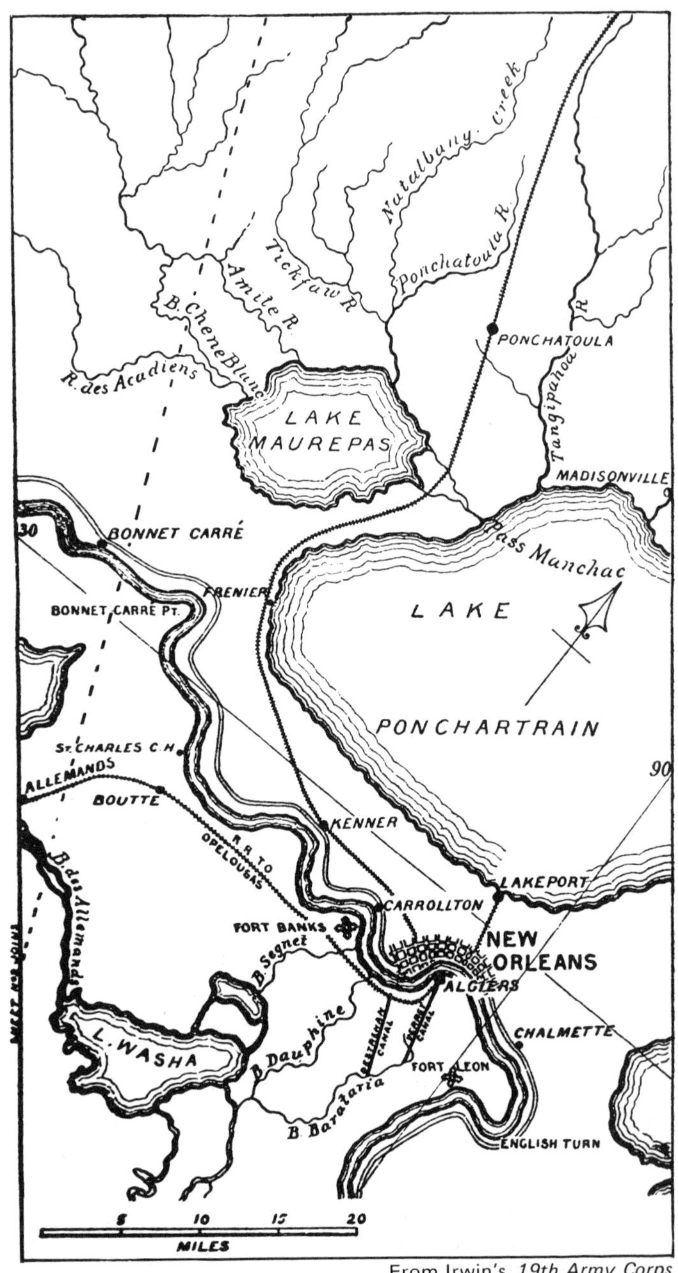

From Irwin's, *19th Army Corps*

MAP OF NEW ORLEANS-BAYOU DES ALLEMANDS AREA

the bayou and by means of abuse of a flag of truce to which they induced an answer and then seized the bearers and putting them in front of their column of attack caused a surrender of the remainder before our supporting force could reach them." He added, "These supports were detained by the unfortunate accident of running upon an ox along the track, which broke up the train and wounded several of the troops."[9]

An interesting story was published in a regimental history of the 8th Vermont Volunteers. It was reported that seven Germans who had enlisted in this U.S. regiment at New Orleans were among those prisoners captured at Bayou Des Allemands. The seven unfortunate soldiers were recognized by some members of the Confederate guard, arrested as deserters, and then executed. The report stated that "the men had protested their utter innocence of the crime laid to their charge and pleaded that the act of enlistment was an exercise of their rightful privilege as citizens of the United States." It was further stated that the captors would not listen or show them any mercy or allow the Germans to communicate with their friends nor make any preparation for their defense. A court martial was then held "which went through a farce of hearing testimony and returned a quick verdict of guilty."

The report continued that the men were marched under some trees beside a railroad track where a long trench had been dug. Here they were arranged in such a manner that when shot they would fall dead into the trench. Seventy Confederate soldiers were summoned with their muskets to do the job but several were unwilling and hired substitutes. However, a blank cartridge was placed in one of the rifles unknown to any of the executioners and when the Germans were shot it left a consoling doubt as to just who did it. The story went on to state that the warm bodies were hastily thrust into the open grave and just enough dirt was thrown upon them to hide them from "the face of the accusing sun." It is mentioned that an aged heartbroken father shoveled the dirt away from the mouldering remains of his only son, a handsome lad, and said with tears rolling down his cheeks, "It is hard to let him go, for he is all that I have."[10]

Taylor who knew the lay of the land in his home area warned Waller to be very careful while deploying troops along the river bank in St. Charles Parish because they could be easily trapped. But Waller, having had immunity of attack for several days, became careless.[11]

Butler ordered Colonel McMillan to take a portion of the 21st Indiana Regiment and Ninth Connecticut and land below Waller's forces and also sent Colonel Paine to take the Fourteenth Maine and Fourth Wisconsin and land above Waller.[12]

The maneuver was executed according to plan, entrapping the entire Confederate force. But Waller refused to surrender and ordered his troops to hide in a cane field. They were unmounted and every fourth man held horses. But an accidental shot exposed their location and right away they became the targets of a heated barrage of gunfire. Some of the horses became frightened and ran off. Waller in an effort to lead his men through the treacherous swamp was forced to leave nearly all the horses and commanded his men to retreat by foot. They finally escaped to General Taylor's plantation and back to Thibodaux, Louisiana.[13] Butler claimed that his men captured 40 prisoners, including several officers, 250 horses and equipment. He also reported that the enemy lost 8 killed and wounded.[14]

But Taylor with his accustomed energy and determination directed his units to continue their maurading attacks in the Lafourche country—an activity which presented a constant aggravation to the Federal forces.[15] Evidently these guerilla attacks were having a telling effect upon Butler for he indicated the following in his report of September 11, 1862:

> "I will endeavor as soon as I receive reinforcements to organize an expedition which shall relieve the western part of Louisiana from the presence of any forces of the enemy."[16]

From Library of Congress

UNION GENERAL GODFREY WEITZEL

Towards the end of September, Butler arranged to have his military advisor, Lieutenant Godfrey Weitzel of the Engineers, promoted to the rank of brigadier-general. Weitzel was said to be a West Pointer, 26 years of age, six-foot-four inches tall and a man of attractive and imposing presence.[17]

The force that was formed for Weitzel was called the Reserve Brigade and consisted of the 12th and 13th Connecticut, 75th New York and 8th New Hampshire Regiments, Carruth's 6th Massachusetts Battery, Perkins' Troop "C" of the Massachusetts Cavalry under Williamson; numbering altogether approximately 3,000 soldiers.[18]

Butler lost no time in directing Weitzel to begin planning a campaign for dislodging Taylor's units from the Lafourche District. He felt that this was not only a security measure for the defense of the city of New Orleans and protection of shipping along the Mississippi but it also presented an opportunity to occupy the fertile regions along the Gulf Coast west of the Mississippi River.[19]

In his report of October 24, 1862, Butler stipulated that an expedition had been organized consisting of a brigade under the command of Brigadier General Weitzel to move upon the western bank of the Mississippi through Western Louisiana for the purpose of dispersing the forces assembled there under General Taylor.[20]

He also stated that he proposed to send around:

> "Some light draught steamers, which I have been fitting for the service by protecting their boilers and engines with iron coverings so as to prevent, if possible, the recurrence of the dreadful accident which occured on the Mound City steamer by the penetration of her boilers by shot and by mounting them with light guns, to attack some batteries at Berwick Bay, to penetrate the waters of the bay and tributaries, and cut off the supplies of cattle for the Rebel army from Texas via Opelousas and New Iberia, and to act in conjunction with Brigadier General Weitzel. At the same time push forward a column from Algiers, consisting of the Eighth

Regiment Vermont Volunteers and the First Regiment of Native Guards (Colored), along the Opelousas Railroad to Thibodaux and Brashear City, open the railway for the purpose of forwarding supplies to General Weitzel's expedition, and to give the loyal planters an opportunity to forward their sugar and cotton to this city (meaning New Orleans)."[21]

He continued:

> "I can easily hold this portion of Louisiana, by far the richest, and extend the movement as far as to substantially cut off all supplies from Texas to the enemy this coming winter by this route, if I can receive early reinforcements."

Butler made a plea to the department for New England troops and especially units from the state of Massachusetts as he claimed that the soldiers from that state "behaved very well."[22]

(Author's note: As a matter of fact the Federal forces that were involved in future action in the bayou country were practically all New Englanders.)

Butler noted that he would be glad if General Weitzel got into a position to move against Texas and suggested that the appropriate base of operations would be through Galveston which had just surrendered to the Union naval force. But he was concerned about holding it as he stated:

> "I have hardly a regiment which I can spare to hold it, although I propose to send one—not that I anticipate an immediate attack upon New Orleans nor that I fear it, unless I am forced to receive the 'debris' of the southwestern wing after the defeat of General Bragg by General Buell, while if I weaken myself here I may invite an attack from such source."[23]

Because of the lay of the land in the bayou country, Butler felt that special provisions would have to be made in order to conduct an efficient invasion. The shallow network of bayous presented a problem since the department

Courtesy of Mrs. Alfred S. Landry

CONFEDERATE GENERAL ALFRED MOUTON

had no shallow draft gunboats to support the land attack. So Butler requisitioned four light gunboats: the *Estrella, Calhoun, Kinsman* and the *Diana.* The navy was to furnish the officers and crews.[24]

In the meantime (about October 1st) Colonel Alfred Mouton, who had recovered from an injury during the battle of Shiloh, was promoted to brigadier general and reported to General Taylor for duty. Mouton, only 33 years of age and a graduate of West Point, was assigned to the Lafourche District. Like Taylor he knew how to maneuver in the swamps and bayous of Louisiana and this new task, much to his delight, reunited him with the Acadians of the 18th Louisiana Regiment.[25]

Mouton was instructed to make Thibodaux his main headquarters and he was to picket Bayou Des Allemands and Donaldsonville. He was also directed to secure early information on the enemy's movements and to provide a moveable floating bridge to accommodate the crossing of troops from one side of the bayou to the other as Bayou Lafourche was too shallow to admit river steamers.[26]

On Friday, October 17th, Waller's unit received a dispatch ordering them to Lake Charles on the Calcasieu River with the assurance that his men would be remounted. This news was received with immense joy for Waller's cavalry had borne the embarrassment of being without horses since the September 8th retreat through the swamps.[27]

Besides the 18th Louisiana, Mouton had under his command the Crescent, Terrebonne and Thirty-Third Regiments, Semmes' and Ralston's batteries, and the 2nd Louisiana cavalry. This represented a force of approximately 1,400 men.[28]

Actually Mouton appearing on the scene relieved Taylor to the extent that he could plan the defense of the Red River country.[29]

CHAPTER III

THE INVASION OF LAFOURCHE

General Weitzel decided to make his big move upon the Lafourche country. He left Carrollton, Louisiana, in the afternoon of October 24th, with his brigade loaded aboard transports and protected by four gunboats. The invading flotilla steamed up the Mississippi with Captain George M. Ransom of the gunboat *Kineo* in command of the fleet. The other gunboats were the *Sciota, Katahdin* and the *Itasca.*

Weitzel landed his force at Miner's Point, six miles below Donaldsonville and directed the transports to continue to carry the baggage and caissons while the column made its advance on land. The Federal general and his force entered Donaldsonville at ten a.m., October 25th, without opposition. This little town which is situated astride Bayou Lafourche still showed the charred results of Farragut's earlier retaliatory attack.[1]

Weitzel immediately sent out the Thirteenth Connecticut and Perkins' Cavalry on a reconnaissance that drove in the enemy's pickets, captured thirteen prisoners, and reported Mouton's forces encamped on both sides of Bayou Lafourche. Weitzel, afraid that a late evening movement would be disadvantageous, decided to launch his attack early in the morning.[2]

In the meantime a contingent of Mouton's troops, under command of Colonel W. G. Vincent at Donaldsonville, had fallen back twelve miles below to the Racconici in Assumption Parish. Colonel Vincent reported that the Union forces had numbered about 2,500 to 3,000 infantry, 250 cavalry and two batteries of field artillery and that the main force was located along the left bank.

Mouton felt that, since Vincent had only 600 infantry, 250 cavalry and Semmes' Field Battery, it would be much safer to fall back and join the reinforcements which Mouton had ordered. The point that Mouton had selected to make his stand was about two miles above Labadieville. The Eighteenth and Crescent Regiments along with Ralston's Battery which left Berwick Bay and Bayou Boeuf arrived at two p.m. on the 26th. Mouton's small brigade received additional reinforcements with the arrival of the Terrebonne Regiment Militia and Faries' Battery on the 28th.[3]

As the Yanks moved southwardly they divided their forces placing approximately 1,500 to 1,800 men on each side of the bayou. Mouton, greatly outnumbered, deployed his forces with 539 on the right bank and 853 on the left bank. According to Mouton the Union column on the right bank pressed on more speedily than that on the left side and the opposite forces met in battle at about nine a. m., October 26th, near the road leading into the settlement called Texas. The Confederate general stated that, even though his forces were inferior in numbers, they succeeded in stopping the Federal drive. But he reported that Ralston's ammunition was running out and his men were so severely injured by the enemy that they were compelled to fall back about a mile and a half below Labadieville.[4]

But the clever General Weitzel was well equipped for bayou fighting. When he began his Lafourche invasion he converted two enormous Mississippi River flatboats into a pontoon bridge and had it floated down the bayou by

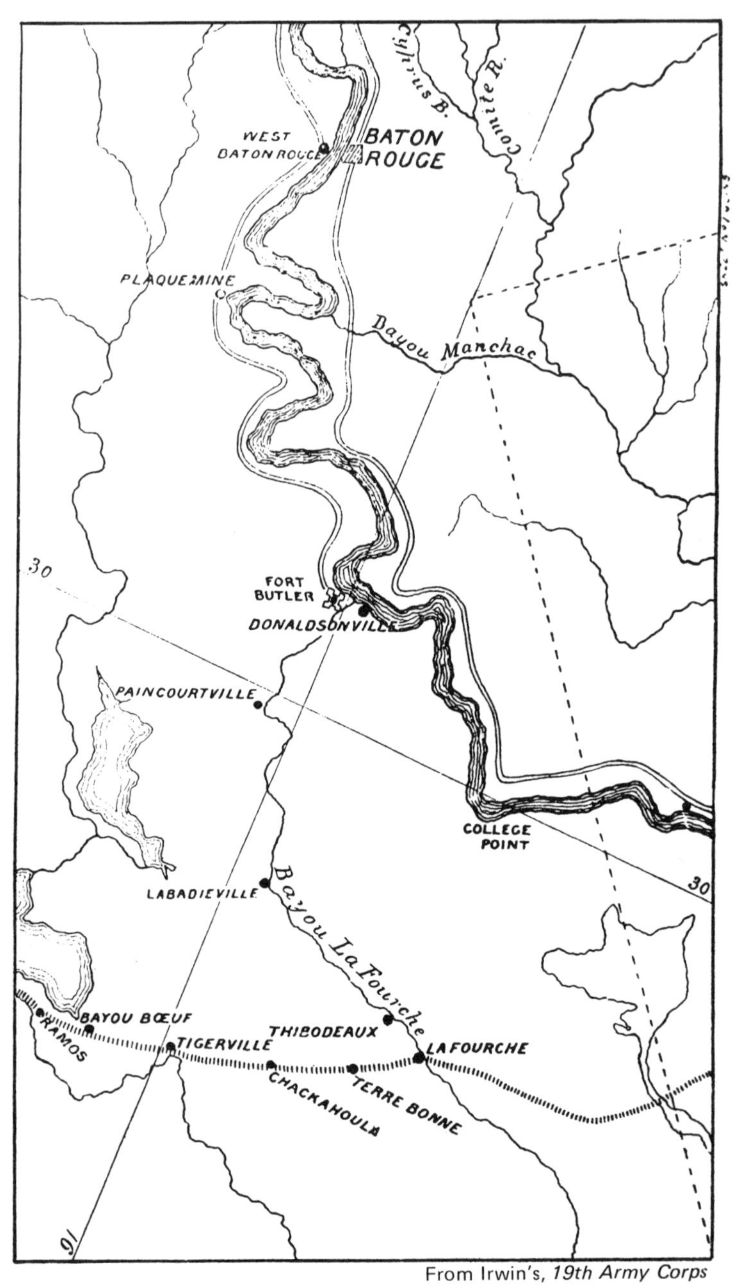

From Irwin's, *19th Army Corps*

MAP OF THE LAFOURCHE AREA

mules and contraband. With the aid of this facility, he now began transferring troops to the right bank, massing his forces for an attack.[5]

Mouton subsequently shifted his troops to the right bank also, but learned to his frustration that the enemy had him outnumbered by over 2 to 1. He estimated that the enemy's line of attack at this point included 2,000 infantry, 100 cavalry and a battery, while his troops barely reached 1,000.[6]

Adding to his unfortunate situation, Mouton learned that the enemy was about to make simultaneous movements via Donaldsonville, Des Allemands, and Berwick Bay. Fearing that his small widespread forces would be imperiled by such action, he decided that he had but one recourse, and that was to abandon Des Allemands and concentrate his forces.

He immediately ordered the assistant quartermaster, Major Sanders, to send over a train to pick up Colonel T. E. Vicks command which consisted of the Lafourche Militia Regiment and the Thirty-Third (about 800 men in all). They were instructed to save everything they could use and destroy everything that might be of use to the enemy.[7]

Mouton also ordered the St. Charles and St. John the Baptist regiments and also the cavalry pickets at Vacherie and Boutte to fall back without delay to join the main body.

However, Mouton's move to immediately concentrate his forces was seriously delayed because of the tedious marches, the time consuming work of destroying facilities and some confusion in orders.

Colonel Vicks' "worn out troops" did not reach Mouton until about three p.m., of the 28th, and Mouton reported that he had no alternative except to maneuver with the enemy as best he could. He ordered that precautions be made to transfer the stores and sick to Berwick Bay.

Realizing that he had the sad alternative of evacuating the place or having his entire command captured, the Confederate commander then directed an orderly retreat toward Berwick Bay.

At about four p.m., on the 29th, Mouton collected most of his troops and while en route to Brashear City, he succeeded in burning the Thibodaux bridge, the Lafourche crossing bridge and the Terrebonne railroad station.

In the engagement around Labadieville, Mouton reported that he lost 5 killed, 8 wounded, 186 missing, while the enemy's loss was set at 250 to 300. He also reported that Colonel G. P. McPheeters, who commanded the Crescent Regiment, was killed in action and that Captain B. S. Story of New Orleans, commanding Company "D," Eighteenth Regiment and Lieutenant J. D. Burke of New Iberia, were captured and later paroled.[8]

In the meantime, Butler had devised a plan which he hoped would result in the capture of Mouton's forces. Four "beefed up" shallow draft gunboats along with a troop transport were ordered to cut off the Confederate retreat at Berwick Bay. The wide expanse of water at this point could certainly make it difficult for Mouton to escape the gauntlet of the Federal gunboats.[9]

Thomas McKean Buchanan of the U.S. Navy led the naval mission aboard his flagship, the *U.S.S. Calhoun.* (Author's note: It may be interesting to mention here that Lieutenant Commander Buchanan was on board the *Congress,* destroyed in Hampton Roads in March, 1862, by the Confederate *Merrimac* commanded by his own brother, Franklin Buchanan. This was another example where brother was pitted against brother in this most unfortunate struggle.[10]) He left Lake Pontchartrain on the afternoon of October 25th, and, as he proceeded toward Southwest Pass, he was met by the gunboat *Estrella* and troop transport *St. Mary's* which was carrying the Twenty-first Indiana Regiment. Buchanan also expected to be joined by the gunboats *Kinsman* and *Diana,* but the *Kinsman* broke down at Fort Pike and the *Diana,* not having her full complement of officers and crew, was left behind.[11]

But Buchanan's coastal voyage was delayed by a norther[12] which struck the general area and caused low tides. He ran aground at Southwest Pass and when his small fleet reached the Atchafalaya Bay on the 29th, he was perplexed with more problems. The Rebels had moved the buoys and stakes which marked the channels and had placed navigational obstructions.[13] The *Kinsman* arrived in the evening of the 30th, and the pilot managed to stake out the channel by working throughout the night. The gunboat *Diana* arrived later.[14]

But the adverse elements that Buchanan encountered gave Mouton the necessary time he needed to conduct a successful crossing of Berwick Bay. He moved everything to the west bank by the 30th, and ordered the immediate construction of fortifications up the Bayou Teche.

The *A. B. Seger,* a small Rebel steamer which had made a reconnaissance of the passes in the Atchafalaya Bay area, returned to Mouton and the officer in charge reported the sighting of four enemy gunboats. The report was rather confusing to the Confederate general so he immediately assigned Captain E. W. Fuller to go aboard the gunboat *Hart* and gather more information.[15]

When Fuller returned, he confirmed the presence of the Federal gunboats in the passes and reported that four of them were visible—two of which returned fire after he fired upon them. He explained that this was his way of finding out the caliber of guns aboard the enemy craft.[16] During this exchange the *Hart* succeeded in striking the *Kinsman* under the port bow.[17]

Mouton actually had only one heavily armed gunboat under his command in the Berwick Bay area. It was the *Cotton* which was a converted Mississippi River passenger steamer commanded by Captain Fuller.[18] The *Cotton* was armed with one 32- and two 24-pounders (smooth bore) located on her bow and one 9-pounder (rifle bore) on her deck. The 9-pounder was cast from plantation bells and named *St. Mary* after the parish in which the gunboat was operating.[19]

The *Hart* and the *Seger* which were already mentioned were lighter-armed craft. These along with several light sloops were also available to the Confederate general.

But Mouton, knowing full well that his meager fleet was no match for Buchanan's armored gunboats which carried rifled guns, avoided a confrontation at this time and gave orders to Fuller for the withdrawal of the lighter units.[20]

Fuller reported that on November 1st, the orders were obeyed by Lieutenant C. Montague of the *Hart* who proceeded up the Teche towing a barge loaded with government sugar and by Acting Master J. M. Rogers of the *Launch No. 1* who withdrew up Grand Lake towards Indian Bend. But the *Seger* under command of Acting Master I. C. Coons disobeyed the order to proceed towards Grand Lake and instead turned up the Atchafalaya. The *Seger* was then "ignobly abandoned to the enemy." This incident happened at a time when the *Cotton* was maneuvering between the enemy and the *Seger*. Commanding Officer Coons was said to have abandoned his men and boat and proceeded as fast as he could to St. Martinville.[21]

Fuller, while directing the departure of the other Rebel boats, came into gun range of three of the enemy gunboats. They blasted away at the *Cotton* and caused it to withdraw up the Atchafalaya River. Fuller, however, even though he was retreating was able to fire one shot which struck its mark on one of the gunboats, killing three men and wounding five. He claimed that the Federals fired a combination of eighteen guns during a thirty minute period before they gave up the chase. When the *Cotton* came into the Teche, she turned her bow down-stream and backed up the bayou keeping her heavy guns trained in the direction of the enemy.[22]

Fuller docked his boat and weary crew at the Turelier plantation for the night.

By this action the Federals succeeded in capturing Berwick Bay, along with Brashear City on the east and Berwick on the west. They also captured the *Seger* and immediately put it to use.

(Author's note: We are careful here not to mislead the reader into thinking that Brashear City was a large municipality. The following is one Yankee's opinion of the place: "The town of Brashear has been dignified with the title of city, but it is in fact, a poor specimen of a squalid southern village, containing not more than three hundred people in time of peace. It is situated on the banks of Berwick Bay, which is about three-fourths of a mile wide."[23] Another Union scribe stated that the town was the terminus of a railroad and that it had a depot and storehouses. He added that Brashear City was the port of entry with a respectable harbor, wharves and a few craft but was what people in the North would call a village.[24] There was also mention that Brashear City consisted of a few houses, a dilapidated wharf and lots of mud.[25] Gouverneur Morris of the 6th Regiment New York Volunteers described the town as a "very abortive sort of a place." He mentioned that Brashear City had attained to the dignity of a dozen frame houses close together and a dozen more scattered along the banks of the bayou. Morris wrote that a Louisiana contraband stated that the town had been "borned and hadn't growed."[26]

But as we go along in this story we will become more and more convinced that Brashear City was perhaps the most strategic point in the bayou country campaign considering its geographical location for communication by land, water and by rail.)

Buchanan anchored the *St. Mary's* off Brashear City during the night. His gunboats, which had floundered in the shallow passes of the Atchafalaya Bay for two days, met him the following morning. But of course Buchanan was chagrined to learn that the Rebels had safely crossed Berwick Bay forty-eight hours before his fleet had arrived.[27]

Buchanan also learned to his sorrow that at Brashear City, the Rebels had run their locomotives into each other and smashed them badly—also that the bridges over Bayou Ramos and Bayou Boeuf had been burned by the enemy.[28]

General Weitzel, while based at Thibodaux, deployed his troops in the general direction of Berwick Bay. He ordered Colonel Stephen Thomas of the Eighth Vermont Volunteers to continue his assignment of reconstructing the New Orleans-Opelousas Railroad which had been damaged severely by Mouton's men. Colonel Thomas, working his way westwardly with his construction train, came to an abrupt halt at Bayou Boeuf, which is located five miles east of Brashear. The 675-foot-long bridge there had been severely burned by the enemy. His men were experienced bridge builders and they began cutting timbers in the adjacent woods for the repair of the long span.[29]

On November 2nd, the soldiers from the troop ship *St. Mary's* landed safely at Brashear City. Among them were mechanics, locomotive builders and bridge builders. They found the mechanical parts which had been removed from the engines and, after salvaging several wrecked units, they finally managed to get one steam engine operating.[30]

As the Federal troops expanded their occupation of Lafourche, many Negro slaves from the various plantations began to desert their masters and joined in the victory train. At Brashear City, over four hundred wagon loads of Negroes were left behind by the Confederates in their hasty retreat.

The presence of so many Negroes presented a problem for General Weitzel. He complained that he had twice as many Negroes around his camp at Thibodaux as he had soldiers and he didn't know what to do with them. He couldn't feed them and as a consequence they had to find food for themselves. He reported that many of the white citizens of the community, who had already taken an oath of allegiance, begged to retain their arms for fear of attack from belligerent Negroes.[31]

Adding to Weitzel's displeasure was the assigning of two colored regiments to his command. Weitzel sent a communication to Major George Strong, Assistant Adjutant General, stating that he could not command these regiments because since their arrival "symptoms of servile insurrection are becoming apparent." He added that "women and children and even men are in terror" and that the able-bodied men were not around to protect them.

Although a new district in the Lafourche-Teche area was being set up with Weitzel in command, he indicated that he could not accept under the prevailing circumstances.[32]

Strong explained to Weitzel that by an act of Congress those Negroes who left their masters in occupied territory were free. He emphasized that it was the duty of the Federal command to take care of them and one way of doing it was by employment. He suggested sending the Negroes back to the plantations to help on the sugar crops for those owners who were loyal and work for the United States where the owners were disloyal. Strong indicated that this was a plan he was using on plantations along the Mississippi River.[33]

In still another communique to Strong, Weitzel pointed out that Major-General Butler's terms to employ Negroes on plantations was not working out so well in the Lafourche area. He told of one instance where Negroes had refused to work on the plantation of David Pugh (located a short distance above Thibodaux) and "without provocation or cause of any kind," assaulted Mr. Pugh and his overseer, injuring them severely.

Weitzel related another incident where an outbreak had occurred on the plantation of W. J. Miner which was located on the Terre Bonne road about sixteen miles from Thibodaux. He indicated that the entire community at this place was in terror of a general uprising.[34]

While Weitzel was "ironing out" his troubles with the Union command, "Dick" Taylor had troubles of his own. The Confederate general was greatly disturbed when he first received word of Mouton's reverses at Labadieville. He hastened to Berwick Bay, where he became even more distressed when he learned that his ace general had retreated to the west bank and was chased up the Atchafalaya River.[35]

After taking time out to make a careful analysis of Mouton's predicament, Taylor realized that perhaps his general had made the right decision after all by avoiding being cut off by Buchanan.

But General Taylor to some extent blamed his high command for causing his forces to be faced with such a bad situation. He contended that if the Rebel gunboats, *Mobile* and *St. Mary's* had not been transferred from Berwick Bay to the Yazoo River then they could have teamed up with the *Cotton* and sunk Buchanan's fleet.

CONFEDERATE GENERAL H. H. SIBLEY

Taylor also made mention in his report to General J. C. Pemberton, department commander at Jackson, Mississippi, that he observed numerous citizens in the Teche country who were removing their families and Negroes and that "alarm and panic seemed to have seized the public mind." Taylor pointed out that nearly all of Mouton's troops were raised in this vicinity and that under such circumstances straggling was apt to occur, causing the strength of command to become materially lessened. He asked for a regiment that would not be subject to these influences.[36]

Taylor inferred that he was disappointed in a change of orders which involved Brigadier General Henry Sibley and his brigade. Taylor pointed out that Sibley was supposed to report to him but was sent to Richmond, Virginia, instead.

(Author's note: Sibley was a native of Natchitoches, Louisiana, a West Point graduate, a veteran of the Mexican War, and had been in charge of the Department of New Mexico. He was the inventor of the then popular Sibley tent, which caught on for a while but was later discontinued. General Sibley was eventually assigned to Taylor's command.)[37]

CHAPTER IV

GUNBOATS ON THE TECHE

The danger of further penetration of Federal gunboats into the bayou country posed a serious problem for the Confederate command. If the Yanks succeeded in their westward thrust, they could soon cut off precious supplies such as salt, sugar, molasses, cotton, beef, pork and vegetables from being distributed to the Confederacy. Salt was perhaps the most valuable commodity, since it was used extensively in the preservation of meat and was an essential ingredient in the seasoning of foods.

Prior to the War most of the salt consumed in the South came from England through the Port of New Orleans. But this access was eliminated when the city fell, and too, as a result of Farragut's coastal blockade.[1]

During this period a most important salt mine was being developed at Petite Anse Island (now known as Avery Island) located about 10 miles southwest of New Iberia. The small island rises to a height of about 170 feet in the midst of a wide spreading sea swamp. Bayou Petite Anse takes a crooked course from the island to Vermilion Bay.

Judge Daniel D. Avery, a prominent Southerner, who was married to Sarah Marsh, owner of most of the island, was developing an elaborate salt evaporating plant, utilizing brine springs which had been discovered on the island before the turn of the 19th century. Judge Avery was dedicated to Dixie's cause and began developing the plant primarily to supply salt to the Confederate States and Army. In fact he allowed a number of Southern States to establish their own salt works on the island.[2]

However, after a number of operations had gotten underway, it was learned that the amount of brine from the wells was insufficient to accommodate the various operators.

Later, in May of 1862, young John Avery, who was the son of the judge and in charge of production, made a most important discovery. While his slaves were cleaning out and deepening one of the salt springs, they suddenly ran across a tremendous rock salt bed. It was the first rock salt discovery in the continental U.S.A., and the vein was only 15 to 20 feet below the ground level. General Taylor learned about the new find through his intelligence and consequently Judge Avery placed the mine at Taylor's disposal.[3]

A great many Negro workmen were then assembled to extract the salt from the mine and a packing establishment was organized at New Iberia to cure beef. During the succeeding months large quantities of salt and salt beef were transported by steamers to Vicksburg, Port Hudson, and other ports east of the Mississippi.[4]

Two companies of infantry and a section of artillery were posted on the island to preserve order among the workmen and to safeguard the salt mine against sudden attack by the enemy.

But the appearance of Federal gunboats in the Berwick Bay area had presented a serious problem for the shipment of salt to the Confederacy. Captain D. S. Pattison, who was sent to the mine with the steamer *Newsboy,* worked up a contract for a purchase of around 200,000 pounds of salt.

The first shipment of 40,000 pounds destined for the Vicksburg, Mississippi area was held back by the blockade.

But apparently General Taylor succeeded in having this shipment transported across land to a point on the upper Atchafalaya and then by steamer on to Mississippi.

However, because of the threatening situation, the remainder of Captain Pattison's contract was cancelled.[5]

The Confederate command, cognizant of the important productive and strategic qualities of the entire Teche area, took immediate steps to construct a strong offense. General Mouton dispatched Colonel V. Sulorkowski, chief engineer with the Engineer Corps, to select a defensible position and erect fortifications. A temporary position was chosen about a half mile up Bayou Teche in the vicinity of Mr. Charpantier's place. Obstructions were then placed a short distance upstream at a crossing known as Cornay's Bridge.[6]

These obstructions consisted of a steamer called the *Flycatcher* and a schooner loaded with bricks—both sunk crossways in the channel. Live oaks were also thrown in to make the barrier even more difficult for the enemy to penetrate.[7]

In the meantime Mouton was preparing a stronger fortification at a more suitable location further up the bayou. The spot selected was Mrs. Meade's plantation which was about two miles above Cornay's Bridge and about 13 miles east of Franklin. Here Mouton was building entrenchments with a view of establishing heavy guns.[8]

This stronghold became known as Fort Bisland named after the donor of a large tract of land for the Confederate cause. The position was well chosen since the line of embankment stretched across a narrow neck of Teche ridge with Grand Lake on the north and a reach of Vermilion Bay swamp on the south. The Teche, however, at this point was open and the railroad embankment to the south served as additional protection for the Confederate forces.[9]

(Author's note: The Bisland area is now known as Calumet. The Wax Lake Outlet, one of the main arteries of the Atchafalaya Basin Floodway project, skirts the western edge of the old battlefield. Much of the redoubts and earthworks was destroyed when the channel was contsructed in the late 1930's and early 40's.)

On November 3rd, Buchanan returned to the Teche with all four of his gunboats and observed that the hastily built fort was evacuated but the gunboat *Cotton* was poised above the obstructions ready for action.

Fuller had been instructed to do all he could to hold back the gunboats so that Mouton's workmen would have the necessary time to build Fort Bisland.

All 27 guns of the Federal fleet opened fire on the *Cotton,* but Buchanan found himself in trouble right from the start. When Buchanan fired his Parrot gun aboard his flagship, the *Calhoun,* he learned that the chocks to which the breeching was secured had broken away. Stopping for repairs he ordered Captain Cooke to move ahead with the two other gunboats.[10]

When the *Estrella* came within gun range of the *Cotton,* Fuller opened fire. The second or third shot struck the *Estrella* on her port rail, killing 2 soldiers who were working on a 24-pound howitzer, wounded another, and carried away the vessel's wheel ropes. The *Estrella* was then run ashore to allow the other boats to pass. The bayou was rather narrow in this vicinity and the boats could only maneuver in single file.

The *Diana* and *Kinsman* then took the lead. But the consistently excellent firing of Fuller's gunners played havoc with Buchanan's fleet and the Confederates cheered as each well-directed shot found its mark. The *Diana* was compelled to stop when the crew learned that the Parrot guns, which were mounted on an iron carriage, failed to function properly. The *Kinsman,* however, worked its way up to the bridge to confront the *Cotton* and also fought off "eleven field pieces" which were stationed on the banks.[11]

During this exchange the *Kinsman* received 54 shots through the hull and upper works and even three through its flag. One round shot managed to penetrate the shell room and magazine but did no more damage than to destroy eleven shell boxes and to knock the sabots off the shells. One man was killed and five wounded aboard the *Kinsman.*

Buchanan backed the *Calhoun* up to the bridge in order to relieve the *Kinsman* which was leaking badly.[12]

Buchanan then ran the bow of his boat into the bank exposing his port broadside to the *Cotton.* Although it was believed that victory was within the grasp of the Confederates, they were extremely distressed to learn that their cartridge ammunition had run out. Fuller, disappointed as he was, slowly backed his vessel out of gun range. But the Rebel ingenuity prevailed. The legs of some of the men's pantaloons were cut off, filled with powder, formed into cartridges and fired at the enemy.[13]

Captain T. A. Faries of the Confederate light artillery unit reported that 1st Lieutenant B. F. Winchester with his two three-inch rifled guns (Parrot fashion) and Captain O. J. Semmes' battery consisting of two James rifles (bronze 12-pounders) engaged the boats for about thirty minutes in spite of the heavy fire of the gunboats.[14]

The result of this day's action found the *Cotton* successfully fighting off four gunboats. Fuller had only one soldier killed, three wounded and his gunboat received very little damage.[15] Even Buchanan reported that the *Cotton's* firing was excellent and that his own fleet received considerable damages. He mentioned that he tried to remove the obstructions by hauling them away and also tried to force the *Diana* through—but all to no avail. He contended, however, that if he had land forces to counteract the land forces of the Rebels, then removing the obstructions would be no problem. The gun battle lasted for about two hours and Buchanan wanted to get out of the bayou before nightfall or else he would be at the mercy of the Rebels' musketry and artillery. He returned to Brashear City to repair damages and bury the dead.[16]

On the following day Captain Fuller resumed his position at Cornay's Bridge where he reconditioned his boat and obtained iron to shield the engines. Buchanan sent the *Diana* on a detail to obtain timber for Colonel Thomas to repair the bridge at Bayou Boeuf.

However, on November 5th the Federal gunboats returned to the battleground at about 10:30 a.m. and Fuller reported that the enemy first fired from behind "a point" and out of range for about 20 minutes.

Suddenly the *Calhoun* and *Estrella* appeared and sped upstream into action. Buchanan's Parrot gun was struck during the exchange, killing two of his gunners. After being bested during the 55-minute melee, Buchanan ordered his vessels to retreat downstream and out of action.

Fuller noted that the enemy had retired and was badly beaten. He made proud mention of his gunman, F. C. Burbank, his pilot, O. S. Burdett, and Privates F. D. Wilkinson and Henry Dorning.[17]

General Taylor in a communique to Secretary of State Judah Benjamin praised Fuller's single-handed action in defeating four gunboats and requested that Fuller be rewarded for his heroic actions. Although Benjamin asked Secretary of War James Seddon to promote Fuller, nothing actually came of it. Adjutant General S. Cooper wrote that the only thing that could be done for the time being was to write a complimentary letter and that, if a vacancy should occur, then Fuller would be named in the promotion.[18]

On the 6th of November, E. C. Weeks, Acting Master of the *Diana,* was on a reconnaissance of Grand Lake. He had heard that there was some cotton in the vicinity and succeeded in finding a substantial amount. He brought back 255 bales and reported that the owners were Union men living in Franklin.

The following day Acting Master George Wiggin was instructed to take his *Kinsman* along with the *Seger* into Grand Lake to capture two steamers which were reported in hiding. After some difficulty he succeeded in locating the enemy steamers up Bayou Chevral about 9 miles from Grand Lake. The vessels were the *Osprey* and the *J. P. Smith,* the *Osprey* having no wheel and part of her machinery gone, while the *J. P. Smith* was said to be rotten.

Wiggin reported that he found a gang of men aboard one of the boats making Bowie knives and molding buckshot and bullets. He wrote that he also found an order which instructed them to burn the boat if the Yankees showed up. Wiggin had the boats burned anyway. He took the captain of the *Smith* and a Captain Caldwell with their company of men and prisoners and turned them over to Colonel McMillan.[19]

In a communique to General Butler, Buchanan emphasized that he had done all he could at Cornay's Bridge but couldn't seem to destroy the enemy. He mentioned that time and time again he succeeded in driving back the *Cotton* and the land units but that the enemy somehow managed to come back strong. He felt that the *Cotton* was casemated as shells seemed to glance off and recommended that he temporarily disband this particular operation until he could receive protection from General Weitzel's ground units.[20]

About the middle of November Buchanan was directed by Butler to organize a force for the destruction of the Avery salt mine at Petite Anse Island. Buchanan ordered the *Diana,* the *Grey Cloud* and the steamer transport *St. Mary's* loaded with McMillan's 21st Indiana Regiment to proceed via the Gulf of Mexico, Vermilion Bay and then up Bayou Petite Anse.[21] (Author's note: The *Grey Cloud* was also known as the *Kinsman.)*[22]

The Confederate command received word of the enemy movement and dispatched T. A. Faries' Louisiana Artillery Units to the Island. Faries loaded two 3-inch rifles and two 12-pound howitzers aboard the *Hart* at Camp Bisland on November 19th and began to proceed to the island by way of the Teche. They reached New Iberia later that day and managed to bivouac 9 miles beyond that town near the end of a causeway which connected the mainland with the island.[23]

This causeway was constructed through a sea marsh and was subject to tidal action. This condition, coupled with the frequent rainfall, caused the road bed to become unusually soft and boggy and presented a problem for the transfer of the field units to the island. The following day after much trouble and delay, Captain Faries succeeded in making the crossing only after he substituted oxen for the six-horse teams in each carriage.

Immediately Second Lieutenant Oscar Gaudet took position on a narrow strip of woods on the sea front of the island with his howitzer section, while First Lieutenant B. F. Winchester stationed his 3-inch rifles on the elevated part of the island.[24]

On Friday the 21st, a small body of Union soldiers began landing by means of little boats. As they approached Gaudet's position, "five spherical case" were fired at the invaders causing them to disperse and retire rapidly towards their boats "dragging with them" a number of their dead or wounded.

The following day Winchester's units also began firing away at the enemy gunboats which were visible in the bayou about a mile and a half away. After firing thirty-three shots the battery commander realized that only a few of the shells managed to reach the target area so he ordered the section to cease fire and secure a closer position at the bottom of the hill. At this time Lieutenant Winchester, who was chief of the section, experienced a close call. As the units began to move downhill, a shell from one of the gunboats struck the ground just where the Lieutenant had been posted.[25]

Satisfied that the Union invaders were repulsed, the Confederate command ordered Faries' battery to return to Bisland. On the 24th the units marched back to New Iberia where the sections were placed aboard the steamers *Darby* and *Hart* and routed back down the Teche.[26]

During the invasion the Union flotilla was fortunate in that a stiff south wind was blowing allowing them to make close approach to the island. But while withdrawing to Vermilion Bay, it was a different story. The wind had shifted to the north causing a low tide and the small fleet was grounded for a period of fifteen to twenty days.[27]

(Author's note: Substantiating the fact that at least one gunboat was grounded in the bay during this period was a report recently submitted by Cletus Cribbs, president of Lake Charles Dredging Co., Lafayette, Louisiana. Mr. Cribbs related that in the spring of 1965 his company had moved its shell dredge, the *H. A. Sawyer,* just off the southeast end of Marsh Island in East Cote Blanche Bay and began dredging for oyster shells. This operation was discontinued, however, when it was learned that cannon balls were being dredged along with the shells. The crew flagged the spot and then moved to a different location.

Later the crew returned with a spud barge which was rigged with a crane and clam shell bucket hoping to find the valuable prize of a sunken ship. But the only things found were coal, cannon balls, Parrot shells, grape shot, and cannister shot. Cribbs was determined to find the reason for the munition deposit and after a thorough investigation received what he felt was a reasonable explanation from a Mobil Oil Co. geologist. The geologist contended that two Union gunboats were supposed to shell Avery Island and that one of the boats ran aground on a shell reef. In order to get more draft, the crew found it necessary to lighten the load by throwing coal and the munitions overboard. Some of the cannon balls were still crated and had markings indicating that they were manufactured at the Savannah Ordinance Depot in Savannah, Illinois.)

The Cincinnati *Commercial* published a letter from a correspondent in New Orleans whereby General Butler was ridiculed for this "hairbrained invasion." Colonel McMillan wrote the general that it was impossible to destroy the mine since it was solid rock salt and not brine which had been used in an evaporating process. The Colonel suggested, however, that he knew of a point where he could load the vessels with cotton. Butler then telegraphed McMillan that "your business is to make war, sir, and not to steal cotton."

The correspondent went on to relate "Among our officers to whom the deep-rooted antipathy of General Butler to cotton stealing is no secret, the dispatch was received . . . . with 'roars of laughter.' "[28]

CHAPTER V

THE *COTTON* FALLS

While the campaigns of 1862 were drawing to a close, the Federal government began changing commanders and turned to the consideration of making new plans. One such change was evident in the order of President Abe Lincoln when, on November 8th, he officially assigned Major General Nathaniel P. Banks to the command of the Department of the Gulf, including Texas, and thereby replacing Butler.

On the 9th of November Henry W. Halleck, general-in-chief, communicated to Banks the order to proceed to New Orleans immediately with troops which were to be collected from the Baltimore area and elsewhere. But Banks encountered delays and did not actually take over his new assignment until December 17th.[1] He left New York with 20,000 men and found 10,000 more in New Orleans including eight batteries of artillery. This was regarded as a pretty strong force considering that the Confederates were scattered in small units throughout the state of Louisiana. It was evident that Banks had his sights set on the acquisi-

From Library of Congress

UNION GENERAL NATHANIEL BANKS

tion of the Red River Valley which included the Atchafalaya Basin.[2]

But Banks got off to a bad start. A few days after his arrival in New Orleans, he was somehow pressured into sending a sea force to occupy Galveston, Texas—a move which proved disastrous. The Union flotilla of two troop-laden transports and six gunboats were bested by Major General John B. Magruder's meager land forces along with two armed steamers which were protected by cotton bales.

The Federals lost two gunboats and several hundred men in the encounter and it all happened on New Year's Day. Although the remainder of the vessels had raised white flags to negotiate a truce, the Union navy claimed that firing continued on the banks where a Union garrison was posted. This firing was regarded as a violation of the truce and so the Federal fleet then put out to sea making it as best they could back to New Orleans.[3]

While Butler and Banks had been preoccupied on other fronts, Weitzel was repairing damages and collecting troops behind Brashear City. But he became quite upset about decisions the Gulf Department Command was making which Weitzel claimed affected his four gunboat strength at Berwick Bay.

In a communique to Banks on January 6, 1863 Weitzel isued a firm protest. He pointed out that one of the gunboats, the *Estrella,* was ordered to Galveston and that Buchanan's flagship, the *Calhoun,* would soon be compelled to go to New Orleans for repairs. Weitzel also understood that another of Buchanan's gunboats was slated to be sent to Lake Pontchartrain to replace the *New London,* which was also ordered to Galveston.

He noted that the admiral had the power to order these vessels because the chief quartermaster had turned them over to the Navy. But Weitzel was letting Banks know that the absence of these gunboats would cause a serious communication problem and at the same time allow the Rebels to attack them with light draught gunboats which were hidden in the adjacent bayous and streams.[4]

The *Estrella* was eventually attached to the flotilla

From the official Naval Records

THE *U.S.S. CALHOUN,*
FLAGSHIP OF BUCHANAN'S FLEET

which was ordered to make another attempt to occupy Galveston—but this effort also ended in disaster.

When Admiral Farragut finally received Weitzel's communication, he pled ignorance to the importance of the *Estrella* in the Berwick Bay area and claimed that Buchanan had replied that he could spare the gunboat.[5]

During this interlude, General Taylor took advantage of the precious time by training soldiers and strengthening his fortifications. He found a spot in the Atchafalaya basin which he thought he could develop into a strategic military post. It was a mound called "Butte-à-la-Rose," located on the west bank of the Atchafalaya River about 12 miles from St. Martinville. In this area the basin branches funneled into the main channel which passed along side of the mound and it was high enough to be protected from flood waters.

Taylor noted that the country between the mound and the Teche was almost impassable as it generally consisted of "lakes, bayous, jungle and bog." Nevertheless he went to work fortifying the mound, erected two 24-pounders and the place was called Fort Burton.[6]

During the early part of January, Weitzel heard reports that Taylor was planning an attack upon the outlying force at Berwick Bay and that the armament of the gunboat *Cotton* was being "beefed up" into an invincible unit. This worried the Union general to the point where he decided to strike the first blow and to do it as quickly as he could.[7]

On Jaunary 13th, at 3:00 a.m., Weitzel began ferrying his cavalry and artillery across the bay of Berwick by means of gunboats, and the infantry were taken to Pattersonville, via the Atchafalaya. This force consisted of seven regiments of infantry, four full batteries of artillery with six extra pieces, and two companies of cavalry. The gunboats engaged in this drive were the light draught flotilla under Buchanan which included the flagship *Calhoun, Estrella, Kinsman* and the *Diana.*

This operation was actually an all out effort of Weitzel

From *Harper's Weekly*

THE GUNBOAT BATTLE AT CORNAY'S BRIDGE

to eliminate the phantom *Cotton* which had terrified the Union forces for so long a period.

After the whole force was reunited, it moved in line to Lynch's Point located near the intersection of the Teche and the Atchafalaya, where it bivouacked for the night. At about 7:00 a.m. the following morning the drive began. The 8th Vermont was transferred to the east or left bank of the bayou while the main line moved forward on the west bank to attack the *Cotton* which became plainly visible to the invaders.[8]

The adopted plan was for the fleet to proceed up the bayou and open the attack to be immediately followed by the land forces as a support. Colonel Stephen Thomas, commander of the 8th Vermont, was detailed to select an officer and 60 men from his regiment as sharpshooters and advance within rifle range of the *Cotton* with the firm purpose of picking the gunners off the deck.[9]

Delays encountered in crossing the detail led by Captain Henry Dutton to the opposite bank and Buchanan's haste in his gunboat attack somewhat "botched up" Weitzel's plans. The *Kinsman* which led the gunboat pack began firing at 8:00 a.m., only to learn that Confederate sharpshooters were stationed in numerous pits along the left bank at Cornay's bridge making it extremely hot for the deck gunners.[10] Of course the heavy guns of Fuller's *Cotton* and crossfire from B. F. Winchester's battery, which was stationed on the right bank, also played havoc with the Yankees.[11]

Suddenly a torpedo exploded under the stern of the *Kinsman,* unshipping her rudder, and then Acting Master Wiggin was shot in the shoulder. The *Kinsman* was forced to back downstream and out of action. Captain A. P. Cooke of the *Estrella* was immediately ordered to go ahead up to the obstruction and battle it out with the *Cotton.* But Cooke replied "the rifle pits line the shore" and made no move. Buchanan seemed incensed by this inaction and told Cooke to move out of the way—that he was going ahead.

The flagship *Calhoun* then moved forward and Buchanan, exposing himself on deck with a spyglass, began observing the obstructions. Rifles from the pits approximately 150 feet away began to "ring out" and Buchanan was hit by one of the minnie balls which penetrated his right temple. The fleet commander flung his spyglass aside, exclaimed "Oh God," and fell dead upon the deck. Two others were killed aboard the *Calhoun* and three aboard the *Kinsman,* with many wounded.[12]

Presently a forward detail of Colonel Willoughby Babcock of the Seventy-fith New York Regiment drove off the Rebel support on the right bank and "shot down" everything in sight on the *Cotton.* Simultaneously the Vermont detail succeeded in driving the enemy from the rifle pits and also repulsed the supporting cavalry. Here the Vermonters claimed capturing 41 prisoners including a lieutenant.

After the *Cotton* was flanked by Union field units and batteries, a steady volley of enemy fire ripped her cabin and cleared the decks. Casualties aboard the vessel began to mount as Lieutenant H. K. Stevens, Corporal V. Gautreau and Privates J. A. Chestnut, O. A. Fleurot and J. B. Melancon were killed in action.[13]

Among the *Cotton's* many wounded was her brave Captain Fuller, who, although shot in both arms, managed to back out of action by steering the wheel with his feet. He was then removed to the steamer *Gossamer,* and transported to Franklin while Lieutenant E. T. King assumed command of the vessel.

Although King returned the *Cotton* to the position above the obstructions, he quickly learned that the Union land forces with their batteries had gained control of the banks and a stand at this spot would be useless under the circumstances. He backed upstream and out of action.[14]

The 8th Vermont continued to move forward a mile or so and succeeded in reaching the earthworks at Bisland which were found to be deserted. But shot and shell from a redoubt across the Teche caused the Yankee regiment to backtrack for cover and they found a sugar house and buildings which they used for protection. Colonel Thomas decided to bivouac in this vicinity, knowing full well that

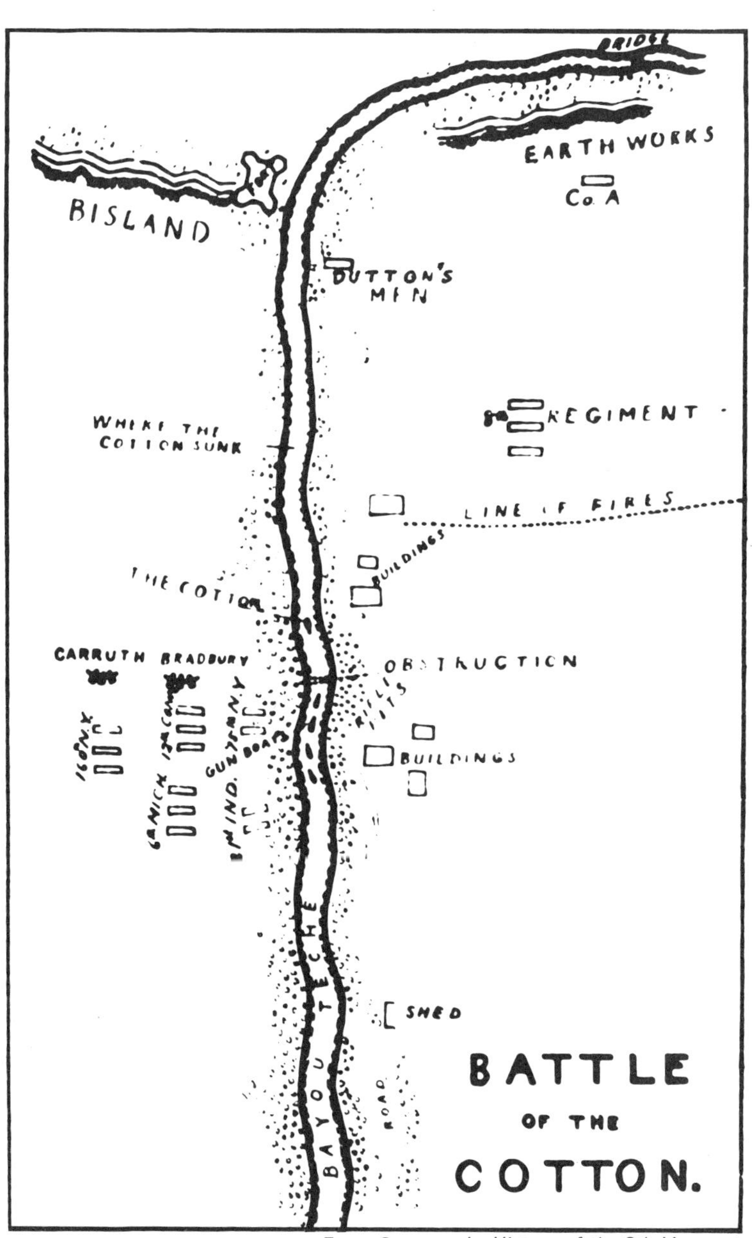

From Carpenter's, *History of the 8th Vermont*

Weitzel's right bank forces were stationed about a mile below.[15]

Colonel Thomas had a brainstorm. He knew that under cover of night the next best thing to being strongly reinforced was to make the enemy believe that such was the case. So under cover of darkness he caused a line of fires to be set from the bayou all the way to the swampy edge of the lake—a distance of about two miles. He felt that by keeping these fires ablaze during the night it would deceive the Confederates into thinking that a large army had accumulated in that vicinity.

At about eleven o'clock that night the dreaded gunboat *Cotton* was seen coming downstream in flames. The vessel had been set afire by her crew and was scuttled crossways in the Teche as an additional obstruction. The *Cotton* burned to the water's edge and was sunk a short distance above Cornay's bridge.[16] Mouton had the two 24's of the *Cotton* mounted in the redoubt on the west bank which was in command of the bayou and the main road. At this time it was estimated that Mouton had three regiments of infantry, two squadrons of cavalry, and two batteries.[17]

The next morning, Weitzel, satisfied that his nemesis, the *Cotton,* had been eliminated, ordered his force to fall back to Brashear City. A strong rear guard was maintained while the regiments retired, setting fire to storehouses filled with corn and forage supplies.[18]

In an article in the Houston, Texas, *Tri-Weekly* it was stated that "the enemy have retreated to Berwick Bay. What are their intentions for the future in regard to this, the fairest portion of our state? The red blaze of incendiarism, the smoldering ruins which mark their backward march, would seem to indicate that they are about to abandon this section and seek to leave cruel remembrances of their fanatical hate behind them. Among the houses destroyed on this side of the bayou we notice those of P. C. Bethel, Mr. A. A. Fuselier, and Mr. Numa Cornay."[19]

When Weitzel arrived in Berwick, he sent General Banks a communique stating that "the Confederate States' gunboat *Cotton* is one of the things that were." This expression carried a spirited ring throughout the Union camps in the area for many months thereafter.[20]

On February 12th, Banks outlined his campaign strategy in a letter to Halleck. He mentioned that General William Emory was already engaged in what Banks considered his "chief movement." This entailed the opening of a water route in the Atchafalaya Basin through Bayou Plaquemine, the Atchafalaya River, the Red River, and then on to the Mississippi. Banks stated that his course would by-pass Port Hudson, cut off the Red River Rebel supply line, and afford safe communication with the forces at Vicksburg. He mentioned that the difficulties in navigation could be overcome and was confident that the strong manned fortification at Butte-à-la-Rose could be captured by Emory's forces.[21]

Banks pointed out that at the same time Weitzel and his forces would be moving up the Teche to intercept the Rebel forces at Franklin and attempt to capture all the steamers in that vicinity. He felt that this expedition could meet General Emory by the St. Martinville road or move to the south of New Iberia and destroy the salt mines at Petite Anse Island. Banks wrote that in conjunction with these two movements the forces at Baton Rouge could move to the rear of Port Hudson and also cut off supplies by way of Clinton.

Banks emphasized that if the enemy supplies by way of Red River and the position west of the Mississippi were to be cut off then the Rebels would consequently be forced to come out of their entrenchments.[22]

Apparently Weitzel didn't think too much of Banks' plan. In a communique to General C. C. Augur, division commander, Weitzel let it be known that he felt that Banks' plan was not the proper one to follow. First, Weitzel pointed out that the banks of Grosse Tete and Atchafalaya Rivers in the Butte-à-la-Rose vicinity were overflowing and that this could not be a practical attack route. He suggested that Emory should join up with him at Brashear City, and, with their equipment and additional forces, overtaking the Rebels would be no big problem. Weitzel stated that Mouton was entrenched at Madam Meade's plantation and Sibley's Texas brigade was reported to be in the Opelousas area.

"I have engaged General Mouton's force twice," Weitzel wrote, "and I think I know its exact strength, condition and position." He indicated that should Sibley team up with Mouton that the combined Union forces could defeat the Rebels in open field battle near New Iberia.[23]

Weitzel outlined the following plan which he felt was practical:[24]

> "Let the light transportation now with General Emory and all destined for and collected by me be collected at Brashear City. Let two of the brigades be moved to and landed at Indian Bend, while the other two are crossed and attack in front. If Mouton escapes (which I think, if properly conducted, will be doubtful) we form a junction at Indian Bend. We proceed to attack and with much superior force (because I do not believe Mouton and Sibley united will exceed 6,000 men). We can defeat them, pursue our success to Alexandria, and of course get Butte-à-la-Rose; our gunboats, to facilitate its fall, attacking it, as they cannot accompany us farther up than St. Martinville. I believe this to be the true and only correct plan of the campaign, and hence these views are submitted."

In view of the activities that followed we can safely assume that Weitzel was instructed by General Augur to make a general reconnaissance of Grand Lake and its tributaries and to report on the topography and conditions which could be considered pertinent information to an invading force.

Weitzel after ordering the *Kinsman* and *Diana* to make the reconnaissance together reported that he had acquired accurate information relative to the projected landing at Indian Bend (near Charenton). He stated that a steamer drawing six feet could get no closer than three miles from shore and that the *Kinsman* drawing four feet was able to get within a mile.

He reported that there were flat boats available and these light craft could get as close as 100 to 200 yards from shore. Although Weitzel mentioned that the bottom of the lake was hard, he was quick to note that he could not ascertain whether or not it was hard enough to bear the weight of his light artillery.

"There is a levee," he wrote, "which could serve the purpose of an entrenchment, about three-fourths of a mile long, just below the road along the lakeshore. The road from the lake to Bayou Teche is good and about three-fourths of a mile long. Where the road strikes the bayou is a ferry. This ferry is a small flat, pulled from one side to the other by a rope. A mile above the ferry is a bridge, the nearest one to the road. The distance from the road to the position which the enemy now occupies below Centerville is 20 miles by road."

Weitzel went on to mention in his report that the enemy could slow down the invading operation by destroying the ferry and the bridge. He pointed out that the gunboats attacking along the Teche must have a force on the banks to clear out rifle pits and to protect the men on board as they cleared out the "serious obstructions" in the channel.[25]

On the upper end of the basin, Lieutenant John Watson, commanding the naval portion of Emory's expedition, found that a raft of driftwood blocked Bayou Sorrel for a quarter mile and a short distance below was another raft of about a mile and a half long. It was also learned that Lake Chicot was jammed with driftwood that had accumulated over a two year period. His recommendations were that it was highly impracticable to transport troops through Lake Chicot, Bayou Sorrel or the upper Grand River because of existing conditions.

On February 17th, Frank Loring, aide-de-camp to Emory, made a similiar observation on the lower end of the basin. He mentioned that the flood waters in the basin were rising and that the Butte-à-la-Rose area was almost submerged and it was impracticable for cavalry, artillery and even the infantry to carry out their objectives.

Loring reported that the *Diana* and *Kinsman* approached within one mile of Butte-à-la-Rose on either side of Cow Island. He wanted to get the *Diana* in closer but Captain Goodwin of the *Diana* refused. The *Kinsman* went the northern route, drove in five pickets and was stopped by sharpshooters.

General Emory was satisfied from his reports that movement of forces via the upper route of the Atchafalaya basin was impracticable at this time and Post Commander L. D. Currie was of the same opinion.[26]

In view of the prevailing conditions and circumstances, it appeared that the Federal command was now ready to adopt the battle plan of its brilliant young general, Godfrey Weitzel, who was highly respected for his judgment in this unusual campaign in the bayou country of Louisiana.[27]

CHAPTER VI

CAPTURE OF THE *DIANA*

The fleet of gunboats in Berwick Bay, under the command of Lieutenant Commander A. P. Cooke, was constantly patrolling the lakes and bayous on a 24-hour schedule. Normally, a detail of sharpshooters from some regiment in the area would accompany each vessel on the cruise.[1]

On the night of February 23rd, a detachment of the 114th New York Volunteers boarded the *Kinsman* at about 8:00 p.m. o'clock for a night patrol. At 9:30 the steamer left the docks at Brashear City and started up the Atchafalaya to Fort Buchanan which was located on the east bank about a mile and a half upstream. When approaching the station a log or snag struck the steamer on the starboard side, just forward of the wheelhouse and suddenly the floating piece was struck hard by the wheel of the vessel.[2]

On investigating the hold, Captain George Wiggin discovered to his consternation that a bad leak had sprung and 6 to 8 inches of water had accumulated in a short period of time. Immediately two steam pumps and all hands were engaged in a bucket bailing operation which seemed to hold the water under control.

Captain Wiggin then ordered the vessel downstream under the greatest pressure of steam hoping to get his boat astride the flats just below the Brashear City wharves. If he could do this he would save the lives of his crew and the heavy guns on board. However, just as he passed the wharves the boat began sinking fast and the gunboats *Calhoun, Diana* and *Estrella* were summoned for help.

The magazine was ordered opened and the powder placed on deck out of reach of the rising water. The *Kinsman* was run head on into shore with her bow grounding in three feet of water, but a 15-foot pole probing at the stern revealed that there was no bottom. A line was ordered to be brought out from the starboard quarter in an effort to pull the boat broadside to the bank. However, before this could be accomplished the steamer filled rapidly with water, slid backwards from the bank and sank in about 18 fathoms of water with all the crewmen's effects.

The *Kinsman* went to its watery grave at twenty-five minutes past midnight with five of its brave crewmen. The other gunboats rendered all the assistance possible in saving the crew and soldiers—otherwise all would have perished.[3]

Earlier E. Kirby Smith was assigned to command the Confederates Southwestern Army which included the Trans-Mississippi Department. His responsibility included the state of Louisiana, west of the Mississippi River.[4] Smith was a West Point graduate and a hero in the Mexican War. Later he served in the Indian campaigns on the Texas frontier and during the War between the States he displayed great ability at Manassas and in the Kentucky campaign.[5]

He assumed control of the Trans-Mississippi on March 7th, and established headquarters at Alexandria, Louisiana.[6]

In late February, Emory's command returned to Carrollton (New Orleans) to await whatever transportation was necessary in order to carry out the movement west of

Berwick Bay. In the meantime Weitzel continued his reconnaissance of the lakes, bays, rivers and bayous.[7]

On the 27th of March, the gunboat *Diana* embarked on a mission which was not altogether considered official business. The stout little steamer, armed with two 32-pound broadside guns, a Parrot and Dahlgren brass-pieces, steamed up the Atchafalaya towing two capacious barges. One of the crewmen carried a document which was purported to be a bill of sale for a large amount of sugar which was to be acquired from the Widow Cochrane.[8]

The *Diana* docked near the widow's sugarhouse which was located just below Pattersonville, and the crewmen began rolling hogsheads of sugar aboard one of the barges. Madame Cochrane, after examining the bill-of-sale, cried out that the document was a fraud. Meanwhile Captain Thomas Peterson of the *Diana* began to suspect that there was Confederate plotting involved in this sugar speculation as the Rebels and the Captain's pickets began skirmishing on the Cochrane grounds.

Captain Peterson feared an attack. Although 20 hogsheads of sugar had already been loaded, he ordered that the sugar be returned to the widow. Immediately thereafter all hands were piped aboard and the *Diana* steamed towards Brashear City, just in time to avoid a well-planned ambush.[9]

The following day Weitzel ordered the *Diana* to make a reconnaissance of the Grand Lake area. The vessel was to plunge down the Atchafalaya to the mouth of the Teche and return by the same route. A detachment of 29 men from Company "A," 12th Connecticut Infantry and 40 men from Company "F" of the 160th New York accompanied the steamer on the detail.[10]

The Federal command was worried about a strong concentration of enemy troops in the lake area as there were rumors that 300 Rebel infantrymen and two field pieces were stationed on a small island in the vicinity. Weitzel sent his aide-de-camp, Lieutenant Pickering Dodge Allen, to gather whatever information he could from the negroes along the way. But one main reason that Weitzel sent

Lieutenant Allen on the cruise was to make sure that Captain Peterson did not deviate from the general plan. Weitzel's opinion of Peterson was that the Captain was inclined to be rash and needed some assistance in judgement.[11]

Captain Peterson went the route as planned, but when the vessel arrived at the mouth of the Teche someone said, "Suppose we go by Pattersonville and give the Rebs a shell or two." Another remarked, "And why not stop at the Widow Cochrane's place?"[12]

This was all the persuasion that Captain Peterson needed as he turned the bow of the *Diana* towards Pattersonville—taking the forbidden route. Lieutenant Allen's pleas for the Captain to turn back landed on deaf ears. Lieutenant Allen then asked Peterson what he would do if he were suddenly attacked by a Rebel battery. He replied that he was not afraid of any batteries and that he could blow up any six of the enemy's batteries to pieces.

It was not long after this conversation took place that Captain Peterson saw a body of the enemy's cavalry and one or two sections of light artillery on shore.

Actually Colonel Henry Gray, the Rebel officer in command, had laid in wait during the night with several hundred infantrymen, some light artillery units and Waller's Texas Cavalry, hoping that the *Diana* would revisit the Widow Cochrane's sugarhouse.[13]

Lieutenant Allen again advised Peterson to turn back and avoid a conflict, but the Captain was determined to continue his course through Pattersonville. When he got within range of a group of Rebels, he "let loose" with his 32-pound pivot rifled gun. The Confederates immediately replied, getting their light batteries in a raking position and the Texas cavalry, now dismounted, began showering lead upon the *Diana's* gunners. The Texas sharpshooters began to take their toll at short range as they picked off the gunners of the doomed vessel. One Union report stated that "No human force might stand up under such a hail of lead and iron as beat upon the *Diana's* decks from every quarter. Her cannoneers were driven from their pieces in the casemates; they scarcely fired a dozen times. Her infantry were powerless, exposed in mass to raking fires. They gave the Rebels a few volleys and then sought shelter between decks."[14]

The Rebel artillery was so well planned that each unit was stationed in such a position as to command the whole surface of the gunboat. Captain Peterson fought desperately and rallied his men repeatedly. The gallant men followed him to their posts, but only to be shot down mercilessly. About a half hour after the fighting had started, the fatal bullet struck the breast of the captain who was standing in the pilothouse. He rushed out shouting "Great God! They have killed me," falling a lifeless corpse on the deck.[15]

Lieutenant Allen then took over and began to retreat slowly down the Atchafalaya. The Rebels became infuriated at this and fired artillery, riflles and revolvers in a frantic effort to stop the *Diana.* The grape and cannister completely cut away the bulwarks of the vessel, while one shot penetrated the escape pipe and enveloped the boat in scalding steam. This created an awkward situation for the crew making it almost impossible for them to distinguish anything. Another crippling blow was that the tiller rope and bell-wires were also shot away. Now the Rebels shouted with joy as steering and operation of the vessel became a serious problem for the ill-fated crew.

Conditions aboard the *Diana* became unbearable. The human gore and blood, the dead and dying were evident in every quarter. This is what a scribe aboard the vessel wrote in his diary:

> "Lieutenant Dolliver shared the fate of Captain Peterson. Lieutenant Allen was shot down soon after. Two infantry lieutenants sank beneath their wounds. Captain Jewett was stricken next. Lieutenant Hall commanded till he fell. Dead and dying strewed the decks. A plunging shot, penetrated double casemating, crashed through the pilot house and Enfield bullets perforated the iron sheathing. A fireman had one leg cut smoothly off; a boatswain's mate received a shot which tore the bones of both his legs completely out. McNally, one of

the engineers, was killed by a fragment which came crushing through the engine-room from a shell which had exploded in the wheelhouse. These strange freaks of violence were noted amid clouds of scalding steam that filled the space below, to which all living men were fleeing for shelter."[16]

The savage battle continued for nearly three hours and Lieutenant Harry Weston, who was the third officer to take over command of the gunboat also refused to surrender. During this period the *Diana* was only able to retreat down-steam a distance of three miles but now it became apparent that the brave crew and shot-up gunboat could endure no more.

The pilot of the *Diana,* a Mr. Dudley, who happened to be a Louisianian, was giving instructions to the engineers below about which wheel to use when a solid shot cut the ladder out from under him causing him to fall overboard.

When he looked up out of the water he saw that a white flag had been raised on the *Diana.* Fearing that he'd be hung if he were caught, Dudley swam away from the scene and was joined by three Negroes who had jumped overboard. The four managed to swim to an island and wade through a treacherous swamp which was infested with poisonous moccasin snakes. They finally made it to the edge of Grand Lake and after seizing a dilapidated boat the party was on its way to safety.[17]

The *Diana* at this point was hardly recognizable. The upper works of the trim steamer were riddled like a sieve from stem to stern and the berths were cut in splinters. Chairs, tables, knives, forks, books, shattered panels, broken glass and china were all mixed in with the bloody mess.[18]

At this sight of victory the Rebels went wild. The lifeboats aboard the *Diana* were riddled with bullet holes but the Confederate officers managed to make it to the gunboat in sugar coolers. (Sugar coolers were coffinlike boxes used as syrup receptacles on sugar plantations but were modified in some cases by the Rebels to be used as boats to accommodate one or two persons.)

Acting Captain Weston then surrendered to Major H. H. Boone of Waller's Texas battalion.[19] It may be well to note here that this was the same group of Waller's horsemen who were demoralized earlier in the campaign when they were trapped in the St. Charles Parish swamp and forced to leave their horses behind. By this outstanding action of the capture of the *Diana* they had redeemed themselves and were proud of the victory.

One of the Texas rangers who couldn't wait for transportation swam to the *Diana* and let out with an Indian war whoop. The Texan then grabbed a violin which belonged to Chief Engineer Lieutenant Robert Mars, jumped overboard and swam to the bank. When he got up on the bank, he mounted a caisson and began playing and dancing to the tune of *Dixie*. Then his comrades, overwhelmed with their accomplishment, paddled out in sugar coolers and swarmed aboard the gunboat to celebrate. Momentarily two Confederate gunboats, the *Era No. 2* and the *Hart,* appeared and joined in the activities.[20]

While the fierce fighting was raging, Captain M. Jordan, commander of the *Calhoun,* heard the heavy firing in the direction of the Teche. Immediately, at 2 p.m., March 28th, he left the wharf at Brashear City with his crew and proceeded up the Grand Lake route to investigate what the uproar was all about.[21]

However the gunboat went hard aground as she was being maneuvered at the Bayou Sorrell intersection.[22] The crew discovered to its sorrow that the vessel had run astride sunken logs and now all movement had stopped. Efforts to loosen the vessel by operating backward and forward were to no avail. The crew then ran out hawsers with kedge anchors astern trying to heave the gunboat into deeper water but this was also an unsuccessful attempt. At 7:00 p.m. the gig in charge of Mr. R. C. Bostwick was ordered to Brashear City for assistance. At 7:15 the four men who had escaped from the *Diana* came on board and told of the capture of the gunboat.

This depressing news "shook up" the *Calhoun's* command, for it was felt that the vessel in its stuck position could fall easy prey to the victory-motivated Rebels. Captain Jordan in a frantic effort decided to lighten the ship by throwing overboard coal, anchors, chain, cable, shot, shell, water, provisions, and other heavy objects. In the meantime he kept his engine constantly working at the kedge anchor. At about one o'clock the following morning the crew succeeded in getting the *Calhoun* afloat and with a deep sigh of relief Jordan returned his vessel safely to Brashear City.[23]

After receiving confirmation of the *Diana's* tragic capture, the commander of the *Calhoun* ordered his boat to be "coaled up" and then headed to Pattersonville under a flag of truce. There they would see about arrangements for the dead and wounded and if possible secure the parole of the prisoners. Although the Rebels stopped the *Calhoun* at the head of Berwick Bay, she was later allowed to proceed on to Pattersonville. The *Calhoun* succeeded in its efforts and returned with 99 paroled soldiers and seamen—also the bodies of Captain Peterson and Master Mate Doliver. But three army officers, three engineer officers and Captain Henry Watson, Jr. were kept as prisoners by the Rebels. Included in this list of prisoners was Lieutenant Pickering Allen who had suffered a serious bullet wound in the left side of his body.[24]

According to Weston, there were 33 Union men killed and wounded in the bloody engagement—seven of whom were officers. He listed the Confederate casualties as 40 killed and wounded. A contradiction to this account was noted in Charles Spurlin's book entitled *West of the Mississippi with Waller's 13th Texas Cavalry Battalion.* He stated that the Confederates lost only one man and his death was accidental, while General Taylor placed enemy loss at 150. Taylor also reported that the gunboat was not seriously damaged and that it could be repaired and placed into service immediately.[25]

The acquisition of the *Diana* gave the Confederates another gunboat in the Teche making a total of three which included the *Era No. 2* and the *Hart.*

The Rebels had also recently captured a gunboat ram

The Queen of the West and General Weitzel was concerned that this vessel along with the ram *Webb* threatened his position. The *Queen* and the *Webb* were reported to be stationed at Butte-à-la-Rose on the Atchafalaya.[26]

Weitzel had also firmly requested that Banks send him all the light-draught gunboats drawing less than seven feet of water that he could find. Weitzel warned that without a superior force of gunboats in Berwick Bay he could not hold his position.[27]

CHAPTER VII

THE BATTLE OF BISLAND

(Author's note: Since the battles of Bisland and Irish Bend were fought simultaneously, it is not an easy task to describe the dual action without constantly switching from one battle to the other—a course which would prove to be somewhat confusing to the reader. However, in the following two chapters the author strives to relate these battles as individually as possible and at the same time maintain the interesting chronology of events as they evolved on both fronts.)

The heavy concentration of Union troops, armament and supplies in the Brashear City area heralded the coming invasion of the strategic bayou country of Louisiana. General Banks moved his headquarters to Brashear City on April 8th but his three divisions of the Nineteenth Army Corps numbering some 18,000 men were hidden from view of Rebel scouts who were posted in the Berwick Bay area.[1]

Weitzel, who had been reinforced by a siege train which was manned by the 1st Indiana Heavy Artillery, had already reoccupied his former front on Berwick Bay. Emory was in bivouac at Bayou Ramos, about five miles in the rear of Weitzel and General Cuvier Grover, who had recently re-occupied the Baton Rouge area, was now posted with his division at Bayou Boeuf which was four miles behind Emory.[2]

Nearly all of the troops which stood in readiness behind Brashear City were ordered to store their superfluous baggage in a large sugar mill located in the Bayou Boeuf area. The officers were restricted to a small valise or carpet bag, a small roll of blankets and those mess utensils which were absolutely necessary.

The mountain of storage which was deposited in the sugar mill was mostly army supplies and extra baggage. But there were a great many trunks, boxes, desks and other containers which were full of watches, money, jewelry and other valuables which were confiscated from some of the southern homes by undisciplined Yankees. Bales of clothing, muskets and revolvers were piled to the ceilings of the lower rooms. All of these items, valued at over a half million dollars, were supposedly left behind for security as well as convenience. (But as fate would have it, the Union forces themselves set fire to the sugar mill at a later date in order to prevent the Confederates from confiscating the precious wares.)[3]

A fleet of gunboats, transports, flats and small steamers had been collected by the Union command at Berwick's Bay and now the time had come for moving the troops to the west bank as the initial phase of the invasion. On the 9th of April at about 10 a.m. Weitzel's division began crossing the bay and while doing so drove away a small party of Confederates who were observing their movements in the vicinity of Berwick. Emory followed Weitzel closely and after both divisions had safely landed before dark they took a position behind Berwick and bivouacked for the night. Necessary transportation and supplies were sent over during the night and also throughout the following day.[4]

A scribe of the 114th New York Volunteers made the observation that an Indian mound at Berwick was used for a signal station. He wrote:

> "Flags by day and lights by night were conversing with another signal party upon a scaffolding from the roof of the depot at Brashear City. There is a mystery in the fluttering of these little flags, back and forth, to the right and to the left, they rapidly make new combinations of movements, till one becomes bewildered in attempting to study their hidden meaning. Wherever a soldier may go, he can always see those black and white flags, waving from tree tops, and roofs, and steeples."[5]

After the ferriage was completed, the gunboats, transports and flatboats were all lined up along the Brashear City wharves to take on Grover's entire division. This included infantry, artillery, cavalry, stores and other provisions which were necessary in waging a battle.[6]

General Banks had now adopted a siege plan similar to the one General Weitzel had suggested earlier. This is what Banks reported to Major General Halleck on April 10th:

> "On Grand Lake, just beyond the head of Cypress Island, and within a few miles of each other, are two shell roads, leading from what are reported as good landings, a distance of 1 1/2 or 2 miles to the Bayou Teche. At one or the other of these landings I propose to disembark Grover, with the object of taking the enemy, who is at Pattersonville, in reverse and cutting off his retreat. The best say that our steamers cannot come nearer than about 1 1/4 miles to the shore, and all our information confirms the truth of this. From that distance the disembarkation must be by the flats which we have collected and prepared for that purpose. Using all the expedition possible, Grover cannot reasonably be expected to land and take up position in less than twelve hours. The boats cannot run at night. His landing must necessarily take place by daylight. To insure this he must leave here by daybreak. The moment Grover passes Pattersonville with his fleet the enemy will certainly take the alarm and if we let night interrupt the landing he will escape. We do not move against the enemy in front today, as I do not wish him to take

the alarm any sooner than we can possibly help. We can whip him in any event, but if he stays where he is, and Grover gets into position before we attack in front, we shall destroy him. Everything promises success. Having destroyed the enemy's force and his salt works at New Iberia, I propose, if time permits, to push a force as far as Opelousas."[7]

Grover in the meantime was having trouble. He encountered great difficulty in loading his guns and horses and was further delayed by a fog which was so thick that the pilots were unable to navigate.

Grover finally got his fleet underway on the morning of April 12th. His division of approximately 10,000 men were jam-packed aboard the gunboats *Clifton, Estrella, Arizona* and *Calhoun;* and the transports *Laurel Hill, Quinnebaug* and *St. Mary's.* Two small tug boats were towing rafts and flatboats loaded with artillery and munitions of war.[8] The whole fleet proceeded up the waters of the Atchafalaya led by the flagship *Clifton.* As the loaded steamers passed Weitzel and Emory's divisions, which had moved out from Berwick the day before, hearty cheers were heard and hands and handkerchiefs waved.

Confederate Colonel Henry Gray, who was now commanding at Camp Bisland, informed General Taylor that a large army of Yankees had crossed the bay, were protected by a fleet of gunboats and all were headed west. Taylor ordered Colonel Tom Green's regiment, Fifth Texas Mounted Volunteers, to proceed to the front, ascertain the strength of the enemy and retard the advance as much as possible. Taylor then ordered the gunboats *Queen of the West, Grand Duke* and *Mary T* to rendezvous at Butte-à-la-Rose and then proceed down the Atchafalaya and Grand Lake.[9]

Weitzel directed Captain H. F. Williamson's First Louisiana Cavalry (Union) and Lieutenant Solan Perkin's Troop "C" of the Massachusetts Cavalry to move well ahead and skirmish with the enemy throughout the day. These units were supported by the 116th New York Infantry and the gunboat *Clifton*. After the Yankees advanced about five miles, the Confederates opened up with six and twelve-pound light pieces which were posted near a large sugar mill. Captain E. C. Bainbridge's First United States Artillery reacted so effectively with his units that he caused the Rebels to cease firing. The Confederates then retired slowly without attempting any serious opposition.[10]

Along the route, the road paralleled the Atchafalaya and the *Clifton* which was in advance of the Union troops continued to shell the woods at frequent intervals clearing the way for the invading troops. The advance became so rapid and so sudden that many of the families of the planters left their homes in haste with valuables lying around. Some of the folk left in such a hurry that dinners were abandoned on the tables untouched or half eaten.

The sugar houses and other buildings were filled with sugar, corn and molasses and Weitzel, fearing that some of his men would confiscate or destroy these products as well as other valuable items, ordered guards to be placed around the houses and plantations. This was protection for the plantation owner who otherwise could have returned to a homeless desert which occurred in many instances.[11]

Pattersonville, some nine miles from Berwick, was reached about 6:00 p.m. and Weitzel rested in line a short distance above the town. Emory, followed closely, bivouacked on Weitzel's left. Besides being responsible for his division, Emory also brought along a string of ambulances and wagons which brought up the rear.

As soon as the troops were dismissed, they broke ranks and stacked arms. Then they proceeded to tear down the rails from the adjoining fences and piled them up for campfires. The banks of the river were lined for miles with men bathing, watering horses and filling their canteens.

A scribe from the 114th New York Volunteers recorded that his regiment camped in the vicinity of where the gunboat *Diana* was captured just 13 days before. The decaying mules and horses of the Rebels which were killed by the *Diana* gave off a terrible stench. He wrote that many of the men, bundled up in blankets around the campfire, would periodically curse the miserable odor and make shouting demands upon the commissary to "remove those rations of meat."[12]

General Banks, who had left Berwick at 4 in the afternoon, joined Weitzel and Emory that night in Pattersonville. The commanding general and his staff occupied a large white house on the right, some twenty yards from the side of the road. Banks decided to command the entire operation of the Teche country invasion personally and had now moved to the front to direct his forces.[13]

General Taylor had around 4,000 troops in the Franklin area which he began concentrating at his front at Bisland. Weitzel and Emory's divisions added up to about 8,000 and as we have already mentioned, Grover's fleet was loaded with 10,000 troops. Comparative strength of the two armies gave the Union forces an overwhelming 4 1/2 to 1 ratio but this didn't scare Taylor. He was determined to stop the mammoth Union machine.[14]

In the meantime Mouton was directed to take over the operations at Bisland and he was making a desperate effort to complete the entrenchments of the fort. Under orders of General Taylor a necessary force of negro workmen was assigned to strengthen the works and they were to work night and day until the fortification was completed.[15]

The Union and Confederate forces were now within close proximity, as Pattersonville was only about five miles east of Fort Bisland. Although reveille was sounded very early on Sunday morning, April 12th, the Union force did not get into motion until about 10 o'clock. The slow down in the drive was intentional, as ample lead time was being given Grover's flotilla as it plowed its way up the Atchafalaya and into Grand Lake.[16]

In an hour or so the Union forces, deployed on a wide front, found themselves leaving the Atchafalaya and were now moving along the banks of Bayou Teche. Negroes along the way were constantly stopping Union soldiers giving them pertinent information about the Confederate defenses that lay ahead. The Yankees moved their line on both sides and brought along a pontoon bridge which they used for transferring the troops. Skirmishes erupted along the way as Rebel cavalry units would frequently dart out of the woods and thickets, picking away at the powerful advancing enemy.[17]

General Banks and staff, accompanied by Generals Emory, Weitzel and Andrews reconnoitered the countryside ahead of the advancing forces, and on one occasion Banks and Emory experienced a narrow escape from Rebel sharpshooters. The two commanders were no more than three feet apart and were discussing future movements, when suddenly from the woods, about 200 yards distant, a dozen muskets were discharged. Bullets whistled past and between the generals, with one ball killing a bodyguard. The attackers were soon dispersed and the Union forces consolidated their lines as a safety measure for future attacks.[18]

The Union forces, unaccustomed to marching through sugar cane fields, found the going rather rough. Because of the war the cane was left unharvested and as the Yanks penetrated the fields, maneuvering through the tangled stalks, row by row, leaping over ditches, they found themselves exhausted and disorganized when they finally emerged into the clearings.[19]

At about 5:00 p.m. after advancing about four miles for the day, Banks' men were suddenly confronted with a barrage of cannon fire as a murderous volley of shells and canister penetrated the Federal line. Banks realized that he was within gun range of Fort Bisland. In addition to this uncomfortable situation, the Yanks discovered that their old gunboat *Diana* was now flying a Rebel flag and it too was hurling Parrot shells in their direction with deadly accuracy. The Yankees were puzzled as to how the *Diana* would suddenly appear around the bend, open fire, and then disappear. They later learned however that it was all a clever Rebel trick. The *Diana* was tied to a rope and when this was loosened the boat would drift out into the open. After her guns were fired the *Diana* would then be pulled back out of sight of the enemy.[20]

After a number of men were killed and wounded, Banks

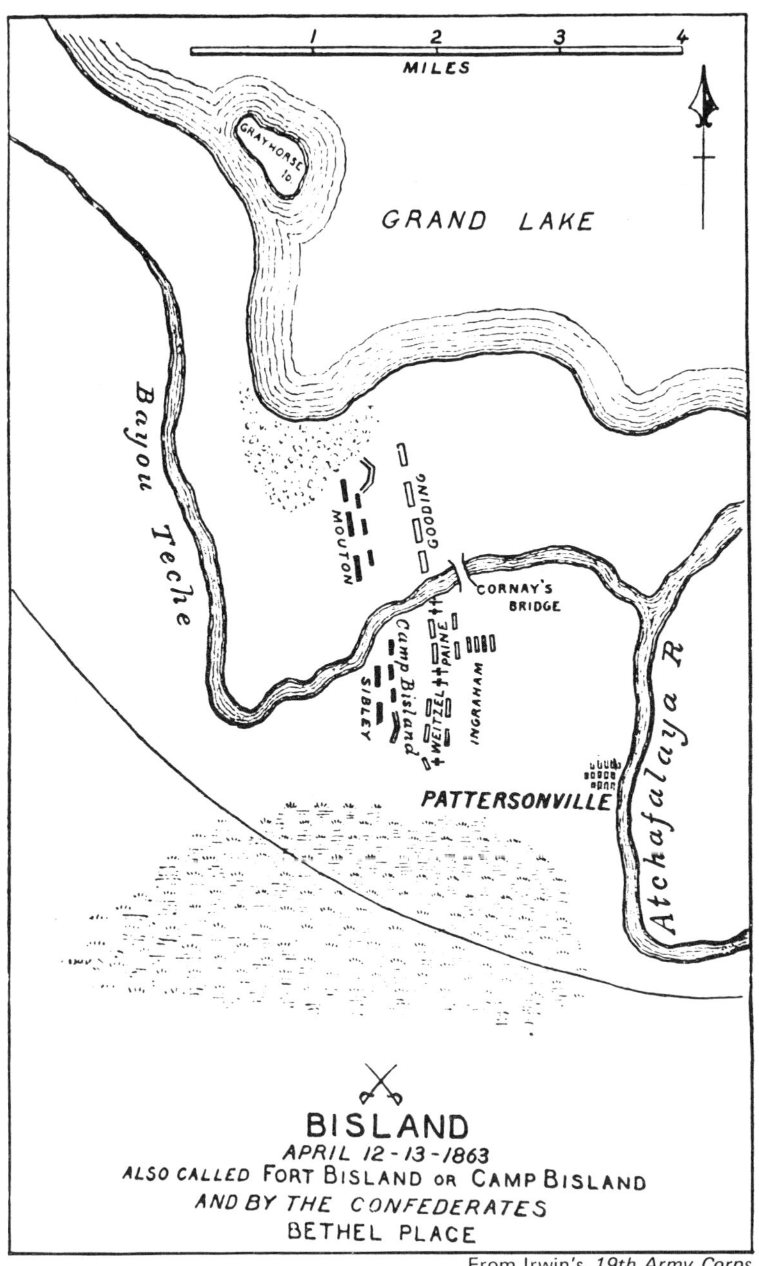
1
2
3
4
MILES
GRAYHORSE IO.
GRAND LAKE
Bayou Teche
MOUTON
GOODING
CORNAY'S BRIDGE
Camp Bisland
SIBLEY
WEITZEL
PAINE
INGRAHAM
PATTERSONVILLE
Atchafalaya R
BISLAND
APRIL 12-13-1863
ALSO CALLED FORT BISLAND OR CAMP BISLAND
AND BY THE CONFEDERATES
BETHEL PLACE
From Irwin's, *19th Army Corps*

knew that he was exposing his men unnecessarily. He immediately ordered them to halt and seek cover in the nearest ditches. The Yankee artillery was then rushed to the front, a hot engagement ensued, and the Battle of Bisland was now underway.[21]

The Confederates were well organized along the entire front at Fort Bisland with Mouton in charge of the troops on the east bank with about 1,500 men and Sibley commanding the forces on the west bank of the Teche with approximately the same number.[22]

The whole force was disposed along the entire line as follows: Colonel Green's Fifth Texas Mounted Volunteers and Waller's Battalion were all dismounted on the extreme right which rested upon a swamp and commanded the approach by the railroad embankment; the Valverde Battery on Green's left with Captain Joseph Sayers in command; Colonel Gray's Twenty-eighth Louisiana Regiment occupying the center, with a section of Cornay's Battery of Light Artillery and Semmes' Battery posted along the center; a 24-pounder siege gun in position under Lieutenant John Tarleton of Cornay's Battery, commanding the road along the west bank of the bayou; the gunboat *Diana* commanded by Lieutenant T. D. Nettles of the Valverde Battery, heading downstream in line of the defenses; and on the east side of the bayou the Yellow Jacket Battalion commanded by Lieutenant V. A. Fournet; the Crescent Regiment under Colonel A. W. Bosworth; the Eighteenth Louisiana Regiment with Colonel Leopold Armant commanding; Faries' Pelican Battery of Light Artillery, posted along the line, and Colonel A. P. Bagby's regiment, the Seventh Texas Mounted Volunteers, dismounted and thrown forward as skirmishers and sharpshooters to the front and in the woods on the extreme left which terminated in a swamp. The Second Louisiana Cavalry under Colonel William G. Vincent and Colonel James Reily's Fourth Texas Mounted Volunteers were held as reserves in the rear of the line.[23]

Taylor was informed by his intelligence that an armed enemy flotilla was sighted in Grand Lake traveling in a westwardly direction. He immediately dispatched Colonel

Vincent and his cavalry to Verdun's Landing, which is located on Grand Lake approximately a mile and a half north of Centerville and about four miles behind the Rebel fortifications at Bisland. Vincent was to observe the movement of the fleet and prevent the enemy from landing.[24]

All over the field the thunder of artillery blended into one continuous roll and sounded to an observer as if a thousand Fourth of July celebrations were concentrated into a second of time. The Yankees were lying in ditches as the men were subjected to one of the severest duels of the war. "The air was rent with solid shot and a haze filled the atmosphere from the smoke of discharged guns and bursting shells."[25]

Taylor, deeply concerned about the Federal fleet's maneuvering in Grand Lake, sent Colonel James Reily's 2nd Louisiana Cavalry (one of Green's regiments) to join Vincent and Cornay. This entire body was then to proceed to the vicinity of Hutchin's Point, which was located northeast of Charenton, and to prevent any landings along that lakeshore position.[26]

The furious battle of Bisland raged for several hours and didn't cease until after sunset. The Union brigade, which was stationed on the firing line, retreated about a mile behind its forward position. This action was looked upon as a sign of victory by the Confederates and as a form of rejoicing the band began to strike up one of its favorite tunes, "Bonnie Blue Flag."[27]

Earlier Taylor had sent for Major F. H. Clack's battalion of some 90 men, which was stationed at the salt mines near New Iberia. He did this in order to bolster his "thinned out" defense. At dark Taylor rode to Franklin to check out the developments in that area and remained there until midnight.

Learning from Reily that no landing had been made on the lakeshore, Taylor then returned to Bisland.[28]

At daybreak (Monday, April 13th) Banks reorganized his line of attack and sent Colonel Oliver Gooding's brigade across the Teche via the pontoon bridge, in order to reinforce those troops which had already crossed. At every advance, however, the Yankees were met with deadly fire from the guns of the *Diana,* Fort Bisland, and the line of earthworks. A scribe from the 75th New York Volunteers reported that the Rebel fire was "so heavy and well directed as to fill the air with flying iron and mow down the men like grass."[29]

Taylor reported that the enemy made two attempts by charging with its infantry but were repulsed with considerable loss by the forces under Green and Gray. He stated that during these charges the Valverde Battery rendered most efficient service and regretted that its gallant commander was wounded. The Twenty-eighth Regiment Louisiana Volunteers, Colonel Gray and Semmes' Battery commanded by Lieutenant J. T. Barnes; a section of Cornay's Battery under Lieutenant M. T. Gordy; and Lieutenant John Tarleton's detachment utilizing a 24-pound siege gun, "checked every advance upon the Rebel center and thwarted every attempt to force it." Taylor added that on the extreme right the enemy was not only repulsed but driven back in confusion through the thickets where he sought cover.[30]

Taylor was also proud of the gallant stand made by General Mouton and his forces on the east bank of the bayou. He singled out Colonel Bagby's Seventh Texas Cavalry, a detachment of the Eighteenth Louisiana Regiment, and Captain Faries' Pelican Battery. He mentioned that Colonel Bagby, in spite of a serious wound, remained on the field until the enemy was driven back.

Rebel Captain O. J. Semmes had been detached from his battery which was located behind the earthworks and ordered to take over command of the gunboat *Diana* replacing Nettles who became seriously ill. We may mention here that Captain Semmes was the son of the famous Confederate Admiral Raphael Semmes of the gunboat *Alabama.* Young Captain Semmes had been recognized by Taylor for his gallantry and "coolness" in action.[31]

Most of the Yankee field pieces were 20-pounder Parrots and the only hope to stave off the enemy attacks was the heavy guns of the *Diana* which consistently blasted away with all their might. Major Brent became quite concerned about the dwindling supply of ammunition and wanted it to be used in emergency purposes only.[32]

Taylor, cognizant that his men were greatly outnumbered and were facing a more powerful enemy force, began to mingle with his troops at the front line. He felt that at this crucial time it was necessary for him to try to build up the men's morale. Mounting the breastworks he lit a cigarette and walked up and down puffing away and chatting with the soldiers.

Taylor mentioned an incident relating to a young captain by the name of Bradford. He wrote that Bradford was perched on a low lying limb of a tree at the front observing the activities of the enemy. Taylor handed Bradford his field glasses and the youngster used these to great advantage. Examples such as this gave confidence to the men who began to expose themselves more freely. Taylor pointed out, however, that his new activity was not altogether successful as some casualties were suffered in consequence.[33]

Colonel Green sent word to Taylor that his men, who were positioned on the Confederate extreme right corner, were subjected to an enormous amount of gunfire and that the battery near him under Captain Sayers was so cut up that it was withdrawn from the front. On further observation, Green came to realize that there were no places on the line particularly cool and there was nothing to be done but submit to the heavy pounding.

Just before noon a battery of heavy guns concentrated its fire upon the *Diana,* which, under Captain Semmes, was pouring its fire upon the center of the advancing line. A conical shell from a 30-pound Parrot siege gun penetrated the plating in front of the gunboat's boilers, exploded in the engine room, deranged a portion of the machinery, killed two men and wounded five others of the crew. This was a disastrous blow for the Rebels as their floating fortress was disabled and pulled out of action for repairs. Taylor reported that the gunboat was lying against the bank under a severe fire and that the waters of the bayou seemed to be boiling like a kettle. Fortunately, Semmes was able to control the outbreak of fires—otherwise, the escaping scalding steam would have driven the crew from the boat.[34]

Later on in the afternoon Colonel Gooding began concentrating his 3rd Brigade to the extreme right near the woods in an attempt to outflank the Rebels. Lieutenant Colonel Sharpe of the 16th New York succeeded in flanking his enemy but the Confederates sent forth reinforcements which staved off the attack. However Gooding sent more units to reinforce Sharpe who made a charge upon a Rebel abatis which was partially hidden in the woods about 200 yards from the earthworks. This was described as a strong position, as the Rebels had dug a ditch and felled trees around it. The Confederates, greatly out-numbered as they were, fought gallantly to hold the fortification, but another strong attack by the Yankees was too much for the meager defenders.[35]

Here the Yankees claimed they killed many of the Rebels and captured 86 prisoners including two lieutenants—one from the Seventh Texas Cavalry and the other from the Eighteenth Louisiana Infantry.

Although Banks was making gains in his position on the Bisland front, he hesitated to engage in an all-out attack for fear that he would botch up his overall plan. He had not yet heard from Grover and as the day wore on he became worried that the successful venture they had hoped for had miscarried.[36]

That afternoon, about 4:00 p.m., a 9-inch shell came hurtling through the air from behind the Union lines and burst over Bisland. This was the gunboat *Clifton's* strange way of announcing its arrival from Grover's fleet. The *Clifton* could not proceed any further than the obstructions and a messenger dispatched the news to Banks that he had been so anxiously awaiting. Grover had landed behind the enemy lines and was marching towards his position.

Banks was so relieved that he withdrew his exhausted units from the firing line so that they could get a good night's rest. However, two of his reserve regiments, the 4th Massachusetts and the 162nd New York were ordered to the front for duty throughout the night.[37]

Taylor still had not heard from Reily and the general's optimistic attitude was that "no news was good news." Taylor felt that his forces had suffered little at Bisland and was encouraged because the *Diana* would resume her position the following morning.

But at around 9:00 p.m., Reily appeared and gave Taylor the grim message that Grover had landed in the vicinity of Hutchin's with thousands of troops along with their artillery. Reily also reported that the Union forces had advanced to the Teche, and the Confederate units, including his own regiment, had been pushed back to and through Franklin.[38]

Taylor was shaken by the adverse information. There was no time to ask questions. The thought occurred to him that if he had to, he and his troops could cut their way through the enemy lines, but he feared the loss of wagons and supplies.

Taylor ordered Mouton to begin withdrawing from the left bank and start his artillery moving towards Franklin. The infantry was then to follow with a rear guard made up of Green with his mounted men and a section of artillery. Semmes was ordered to speed up repairs on the *Diana* and to have the gunboat ready for action by dawn in the vicinity of Franklin.

Taylor then hastened with Reily in the direction of Franklin and found Reily's men asleep three miles below the town. These troops were immediately aroused and ordered to move with their trains towards Franklin.

Taylor then began a nighttime reconnaisance trying to determine how far the enemy had advanced since the time it had landed on the shores of Grand Lake. He arrived in Franklin around 2:00 a.m., and found the village as "silent as the grave." But behind the town he did notice campfires adjacent to a field road often referred to as a "cut-off" road which led in the general direction of New Iberia. Cautiously investigating these fires he found to his delight that they were those of Major F. H. Clack with his Confederate unit which had arrived from New Iberia, to support Taylor at Bisland.

Clack's men were immediately ordered to take up their arms and follow Taylor in his nighttime reconnoitering. Taylor found that the bridge across the Yokely Bayou was still safe and after cautiously advancing through a wooded area above Franklin discovered that the enemy was encamped at the far edge of the cane fields.[39]

Taylor rejoiced that Grover had fallen short of his prize for in another 30 minutes the Federal forces would have easily occupied the field road including the Yokely bridge and consequently Taylor would have been trapped.

The Confederate general placed his artillery on the main road which paralleled the Teche. Reily, Vincent, and Clack's troops formed a line from the guns westwardly to the edge of the woods. All stood fast in preparation of the powerful Yankee attack which was expected at dawn.[40]

CHAPTER VIII

THE BATTLE OF IRISH BEND

At the conclusion of the preceeding chapter we established that Grover had landed behind Taylor's line and that Taylor, just before dawn on April 14, 1863, had positioned some of his forces above Franklin as a line of defense. The author felt that it would certainly be in order at this time to backtrack a few days so that the reader may become better informed about the activities of General Grover as his flotilla maneuvered in the vicinity of Grand Lake.

On the morning of April 12th, as we had explained earlier, Grover's fleet separated from the Bisland-bound troops of Weitzel and Emory, and steamed up the Atchafalaya river to its destination. All vessels were loaded beyond capacity. Giving the reader an idea how jam-packed some of the vessels were, James Hosmer, of the 52nd Massachusetts Volunteers who was aboard the transport *St. Mary's,* compared the packing of his ship with that of a slaver. He wrote:[1]

> "Our boat carried three regiments, the horses and greater part of the men of a battery and I know not

how many more. I only know I took my post on a little rise in the deck, between the smoke-stack and engine, built up to cover the machinery. By daylight, we sat with our legs curled under us under a blazing hot sun, under which we almost popped out on the deck like kernels of corn on an iron plate. By night, we tried to sleep, with the plunging piston within reach of the hand. I lay with my head lower than my feet, my head on my knapsack, my feet passed up over the shoulders of Grider and another of our fellows, with Callihan's elbow in one side, and Bivin's head upon my breast."

Hosmer added that he had slept on what felt like four or five uncovered muskets and when he awoke in the morning he looked like a tattooed "Carib" where the steel projections had pressed into his back and legs.

Hosmer related that during their confinement aboard the vessel the men became in dire need of coffee. One Joe Pray, however, came to the rescue as he figured a novel way in which to make hot coffee. Nearby was the escape-pipe of the steamer which rose ten to twelve feet above the deck from which hot steam was constantly emerging. Pray had a brainstorm. He poured a handful of coffee into his canteen and partly filled it with water. Then he managed to toss the canteen into the current of steam holding the container by a long white string. In a few minutes he withdrew the canteen which was steaming with the hot refreshing drink. Immediately coffee-makers sprung up all over the ship as Pray's system was copied. From that day forward Joe Pray was looked upon as a hero and a genius.[2]

Another observation of the crowded steamer *St. Mary's* was made by Major Thomas McManus of the 25th Connecticut who was aboard with his regiment. He reported that the ship was built to carry 500 persons "at a pinch." On this occasion, however, the major reported that the ship was loaded with 2,500 passengers.

He wrote the following:[3]

"We were crowded. We were just packed as close as the squares of hardtack in the bread barrels, closer than sardines in a box. So close that we didn't have room to sweat. We had to hold our haversacks that contained three days ration of sheet-iron biscuit and salt pork, on our heads. The decks were covered with a solid mass of humanity."

As the invasion-bound fleet plowed its way across Grand Lake, Grover discovered that one of his gunboats had encountered trouble. The *Arizona,* loaded with the 41st Massachusetts Regiment, had run aground at Cypress Pass, and no amount of tugging could budge the ship. Grover immediately transferred 400 men onto the *Clifton* and still no movement could be made. The general was getting impatient, as this delay boded no good for the expedition. After informing the captain of the *Arizona* that it was important that the fleet should proceed without the ground craft, Grover left a few lighters and then steamed away to his destination.[4]

A pontoon bridge was constructed from the lighters and the rest of the men on board the *Arizona* were landed on Cypress Island. The ground troops quickly attached hawsers to the ship and began to tug for "dear life." Still no movement. Adding to the frustration of the stranded men were the dismal sounds of the raging battle of Bisland which could be heard in the distance.

The *Arizona* was grounded at about 11:00 a.m., and at midnight the worn-out crew gave up. The following morning the men made another desperate effort and the ship came out of the mud. At 8:00 a.m., all were aboard and headed west to meet the rest of the fleet.[5]

The preceeding night at about 7:30 o'clock Grover's gunboats and transports anchored below Miller's Point, off Madam Porter's plantation. Grover sent Lieutenant Colonel William Fiske with his two companies of the 1st Louisiana Infantry (Union), who were aboard the *Clifton,* to check out a certain road. About midnight the group returned reporting that the road was under water and impractical to use. The fleet then got underway again and after proceed-

From *Campfires and Battlefields*

LANDING OF FEDERAL FORCES AT INDIAN BEND

ing about six miles farther up the lake, anchored beyond Magee's Point.[6]

Before daylight April 13th, General William Dwight, Jr., Commanding the First Brigade sent two of his staff officers, Captain W. J. Denslow and Lieutenant Oliver Matthews, with a small detachment from the 6th New York Infantry to examine the plantation road which led from Grand Lake to the Teche. The men found this road to be practicable for all arms and at dawn the brigade commenced its debarkation.[7]

Vincent's Cavalry and Cornay's St. Mary Cannoneers, which were dispatched by Taylor earlier to prevent any landings by the enemy, were having a difficult time trying to keep abreast of Grover's fleet. The Rebel units had a long shoreline to watch and the Union flotilla moved more rapidly on the lake than the Confederates could by the roads.[8]

Because of the deep draught of the vessels, Grover's flotilla was unable to get within 100 yards of the shoreline. Dwight was ordered to send his first brigade ashore to dislodge a Rebel force estimated at between 300 and 400 men with a section of artillery. They were Vincent's and Cornay's units partially hidden in a strip of woods which skirted the lake.

Immediately the First Louisiana Regiment under Colonel Richard Holcomb jumped overboard and scrambled towards shore. As soon as Holcomb's invaders reached land they were fired upon by the Rebel units which were positioned behind a high fence in the thickets along the Duncan McWilliams plantation.[9] The gunboat *Clifton* was signalled to fire away and as it began raking the shoreline thickets, Holcomb's skirmishers pressed forward. The Rebels at this point had no other recourse but to fall back to a safe position and they retired to the vicinity of Madam Porter's plantation located about two miles southeast of the landing.[10]

Grover was not too anxious to chase the Rebels at this stage for fear of exposing his brigade to a superior force. Grover preferred to land all of his forces and then begin an all-out-drive. However, he did allow Dwight to detach a small force which consisted of a regiment of infantry and two sections of artillery to proceed to the Bayou Teche and prevent the Rebels from destroying bridges.[11]

The landing of General Grover's division was not an easy undertaking. Foot soldiers presented no problem as they easily scrambled ashore and it was not too difficult to coax the horses through the mud and water. But guns, caissons and other heavy equipment required special attention—so much so, that the general found it necessary to construct a bridge out of flats. This caused considerable delay. The *Clifton,* which unloaded its troops earlier, left for Bisland to deliver the message that Grover had landed.[12]

In the meantime Grover learned through his intelligence that Taylor had dispatched a courier to Butte-à-la-Rose ordering the *Queen of the West* and other available gunboats to move down the lake and attack Grover by water. He also learned that besides Vincent and Cornay's troops another regiment (Clack's) was sent from New Iberia to confront the invaders.[13]

Vincent's forces decided to stave off the Union drive by destroying the Teche bridges. They succeeded in destroying the span which led from McWilliams plantation and also set fire to Madame Porter's bridge a short distance to the east.[14] At about 11:30 a.m., Cornay's Battery was ordered to Bethel's Bridge which was found burning but not completely destroyed and then on to Simon's Bridge which was sunk with the assistance of a Mr. Dillon, who was the manager of Simon's plantation. During these activities shots were exchanged between Dwight's advance attachment and Vincent's men but shortly thereafter a gun from the enemy artillery opened up at long range.[15]

Feeling that he had somewhat hindered the Yankee drive, Vincent then ordered his meager forces to retire towards Franklin. He met Reily with reinforcements about a mile above Franklin.[16]

When Dwight's cavalry reached the Teche, it occupied the junction of the McWilliams road with the north-bank road of the Teche. The Union soldiers extinguished the fire at Madame Porter's bridge before any great damage was done and quickly gathered Negroes from nearby plantations to repair the bridges. Dwight reported that he managed to save two of the bridges and kept possession of the spans while awaiting further orders from the brigadier general.[17]

It was not until about four o'clock in the afternoon that the whole of Grover's division and equipment had landed.[18] Since Grover had no train and only a few wagons carrying ammunition, he decided to issue as much hard bread and coffee as could be carried in haversacks and return the rest of the supplies to the transports.[19] He finally got his division marching in full swing at about 6:00 p.m., and when his men reached the Teche they crossed on the upper two bridges which had been repaired. The division was then routed to the east along the south Teche road and, after marching a short distance past Madame Porter's beautiful mansion (now known as Oaklawn Manor), the brigadier general decided to bivouac in the vicinity for the night.

Madame Porter was heralded as the proprietress of one of the richest plantations in the south, owning several square miles of fertile farm lands, a sugar mill and over 400 slaves. The mansion was located about a half-mile north of the road, facing the Teche and was placed under immediate protection by a detail of the 52nd Massachusetts Infantry Regiment.[20]

The reader is asked at this point to picture the Teche country as being one long, narrow, winding ridge extending in an eastwardly and westwardly direction. In the center of this ridge flows the Bayou Teche with roads on both sides. To the north are Grand Lake and the rest of the Atchafalaya Basin. On the south are peninsulas, marshes, bays and the Gulf of Mexico. North of Franklin, the Teche forms a sort of horseshoe.[21] Located near the curved end of the horseshoe is Madame Porter's mansion. The east leg extends in the direction of Franklin while the other leads to Baldwin. It may be well to mention here that Alexander Porter, who was a U.S. Senator, built the mansion in 1838,

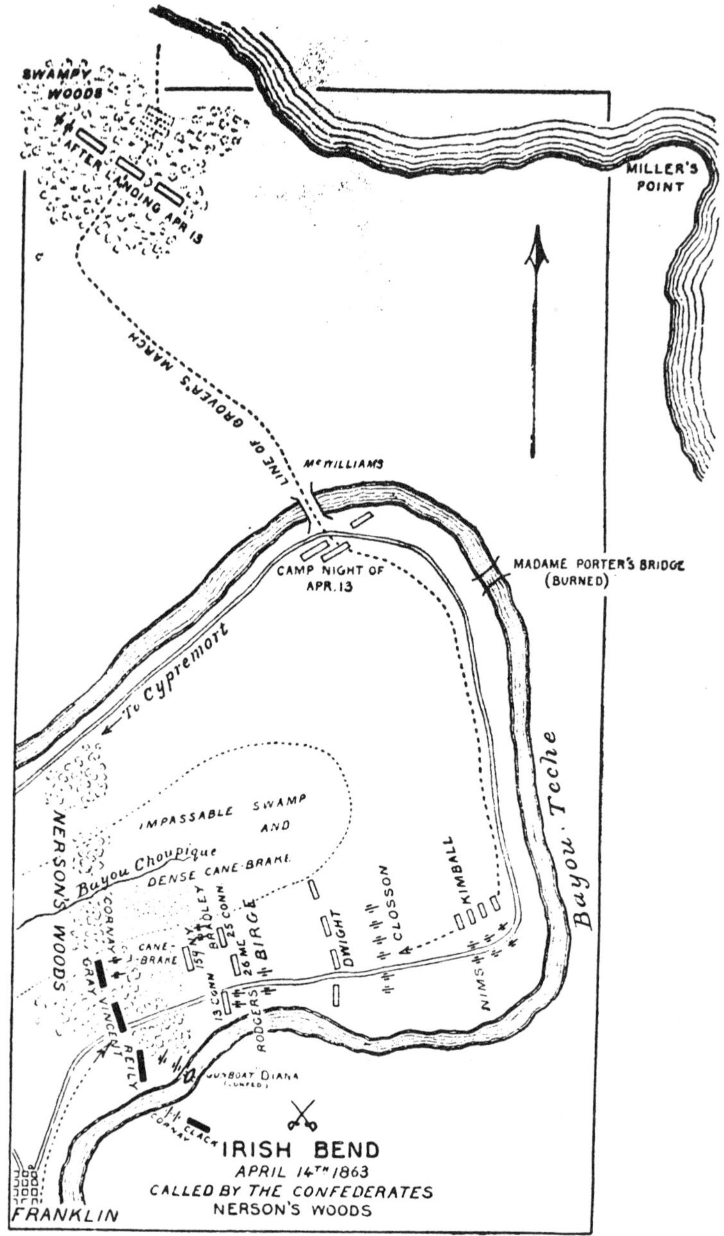
SWAMPY WOODS
AFTER LANDING APR 13
MILLER'S POINT
LINE OF GROVER'S MARCH
McWILLIAMS
CAMP NIGHT OF APR. 13
MADAME PORTER'S BRIDGE (BURNED)
To Cypremort
Bayou Teche
IMPASSABLE SWAMP AND DENSE CANE-BRAKE
Bayou Choupique
NERSON'S WOODS
KIMBALL
CLOSSON
DWIGHT
BIRGE
BRADLEY
25 CONN
159 N.Y.
26 ME
13 CONN
RODGERS
NIMS
CANE-BRAKE
CORNAY
GRAY
VINCENT
REILY
GUNBOAT DIANA
CLACK
CORNAY
FRANKLIN
IRISH BEND
APRIL 14TH 1863
CALLED BY THE CONFEDERATES
NERSON'S WOODS

From Irwin's, *19th Army Corps*

and purchased thousands of acres of land on both sides of the Teche.[22] Porter was an Irishman and steamboat captains probably referred to the curve around Porter's plantation as Irishman's Bend. Later the area took on the abbreviated monicker of Irish Bend.

General Grover was pondering his next move as he sat astride his horse near a road intersection. Suddenly a lank grizzled soldier from Company "H" (52nd Massachusetts Regiment) carrying a musket on his shoulder, appeared with the queenly Madame Porter. She was described as a beautiful woman in her late forties—elegantly dressed and bareheaded. She stopped at the stirrups of General Grover and began pleading for the life of her son who had just been taken prisoner.

"Please let him go, General," she begged. "The poor boy was quite innocent." She continued, "Please let him go, General—he is all I have." She repeated this over and over again.[23]

The General never uttered a word. It appeared that he refused to listen. The son, a tall, fierce-looking young man of about 19 or 20 stood close by under guard. Presently the same grizzled soldier escorted the disappointed lady back to her home.

Colonel Henry Birge of the Thirteenth Connecticut Infantry who was in command of the Third Brigade was ordered by Grover to organize his forces for an attack towards Franklin at dawn.

The following morning, Tuesday, April 14, 1863, brings us up to the time we left Taylor with his men hidden around a cane field at a place called Nerson's Woods located about a mile and a half above Franklin.

Taylor's forces at Nerson's Woods were estimated at around 1,200 men, while Grover's division, as we established earlier, was about 10,000 strong.[24]

At daylight Birge's brigade began to march down the winding road of Franklin in the following order: The 25th Connecticut with five companies as skirmishers deployed to the front from the roads to the bayou and on the right flank, and five companies in reserve in the opening be-

From *Campfires and Battlefields*

BATTLE OF IRISH BEND

tween the woods and the road; two companies of the 26th Maine in the road; first section of Rodger's Battery; eight companies 26th Maine Regiment; 159th New York Regiment; the remainder of Rodger's Battery; and the Thirteenth Connecticut Regiment.[25]

After these troops had marched about two miles and were approaching a right angle turn in the road, near what is now known as Belleview Country Club, the advance skirmishers on the right discovered Rebels who were partially hidden at the edge of the woods across the field. Brisk firing commenced on both sides as Birge's men ran into Clack's battalion near McKerall's sugar house and this action marked the beginning of an engagement which was recorded in history as "The Battle of Irish Bend."[26]

Learning that Taylor was making a stand came as a surprise and big disappointment to the Union generals who felt that once the road in Taylor's rear was occupied by the Yanks, the Confederate general would submit to the inevitable and surrender. But this was certainly not the case for Taylor was a fighter and a strategist—and was not about to surrender.[27]

Between Birge and the concealed Confederate ranks lay the broad and open fields of McKerall's plantation where the young sugar cane stood a foot high, above the deep and wide furrows. On the Union right was the upper basin of Bayou Yokely which was thickly overgrown, swampy and nearly impassable while in front there was a deep transverse ditch which conveyed the drainage waters from the smaller field ditches to the Yokely.[28] Along the western edge of the cane field stood a strip of Nerson's Woods where, as yet unseen by the Yanks, a force of Rebels was shielded even further from view by a low fringe of cane brake and under growth.

The fact that the field was soft with recent rains and had deep furrows made it rather difficult for the movement of both men and guns. But when Birge discovered the position of the Rebels from the musket sounds and gun smoke, he immediately ordered the reserved batallion of the 25th

Connecticut across the field to attack the Confederates' left.[29]

As the Connecticut regiment moved forward, the 159th New York Infantry was brought into line on its left while the 26th Maine formed in the rear. The 13th Connecticut took position on the extreme left advancing down both sides of the Franklin road with its line stretched as far left as the Bayou Teche. Rodger's artillery took a position near the road shelling the woods while General Grover was riding alongside Birge giving orders.[30]

The 25th Connecticut halted about 150 yards from a fence which bordered the woods and a hot exchange of gunfire erupted, causing all the Yankee units in that vicinity to lie down in the furrows and ditches seeking cover as best they could. In this section of the field was unharvested sugar cane of the previous year's crop and the Rebels shots "rattled through the dry stalks like hail against the windows." Major Thomas McManus of the 25th Connecticut reported that the Rebels were armed with the smooth bores where every cartridge was charged with a bullet and three buckshots, while his regiment was armed with Enfield rifles. He inferred that each Rebel shot that was fired produced in reality four bullets which were showered upon his men as compared to a single bullet from each Yankee rifle shot.[31]

General Taylor heard to his delight "the peculiar whistle of a Parrot shell" which meant that Semmes had arrived in the bayou with the *Diana*. Colonel Gray's regiment also arrived around 7:00 a.m. as reinforcement. The *Diana* and Cornay's St. Mary Volunteers began blasting away at the enemy with a continuous volley of shot and shell.[32]

All of the Federal units met with stonewall resistance along the entire front except the 13th Connecticut which managed to penetrate a belt of woods near the road. The Connecticut unit, though startled by the constant cannonading, attacked a force of Rebels in a fashion known as "firing while advancing in line of battle"—considered a difficult though effective tactic.[33]

Casualties began to mount on both sides. The sun getting higher, the soldiers in the field warmed up to their work. Canteens were drained, the men were thirsty and generally exposed to the Rebel fire. Suddenly there were loud Rebel shouts from all around the field, described by some as "wild-cat yells," followed by a constant firing of muskets and cannon. Taylor's men charged from behind fences and trees and startled the "Feds" to no end. A constant roar of gunfire prevailed. One observer claimed that it sounded like a never-ending peal of rolling thunder. About 50 of the 13th Connecticut Regiment fell in the first three minutes of the attack and all the horses of Birge's staff officers were killed or wounded.[34]

One of the units caught in the Confederate crossfire was the 25th Connecticut and Major McManus made the following report: "Another roar, a crack, an iron shower and we see to our dismay two brazen guns admirably served, trained directly upon us pouring shell grape and canister into our ranks while their musketry fire grew hotter and fiercer than ever. Our men were nearing the end of their supply of ammunition. If the Confederates had charged upon us at this time, they would have annihilated our brigade!"

He stated that the wounded men were crawling to the rear to the yellow hospital flag where they would be attended to by the doctor and his assistants. Hosmer of the 52nd Massachusetts gave the following eye-witness report:[35]

> "Ambulance-men with stretchers are hurrying across the field to a sugarhouse in the rear, where a hospital is established. (Author's note: He probably had reference to McKerall's sugar mill.) On each stretcher is a wounded man and the number of these makes it certain to us that the engagement has reached the sad dignity of a pitched battle. We are passing ammunition wagons now; now a tree, beneath which is a surgeon at work, and close where he stands, on his back, stiff and stark, dead, a tall, broad-chested man, with closed eyes. The column files to the right, out of the road; and we stand in line of battle just in the rear of the action, within rifle range of the woods where the enemy is concealed.

> . . . Between the color-company and the next company, through the center of our line, runs the cart track down into the field, along which now is constantly passing a stream of wounded men on stretchers or supported by comrades, and lines of Rebel prisoners. I am close by, and can hear the talk of a sergeant, bloody, but able to walk, who is glad he has had a chance to do some service. I look, too, upon the ghastly head of a young lieutenant who is dying upon his stretcher, and many others. Prisoners came by in squads—sometimes five or six, sometimes twenty or thirty; some in blue, some in faded brown."

When Bradley's artillery arrived at a gallop, Colonel Bissell tried to rally the Connecticut unit but his efforts were in vain.

Suddenly Dwight's brigade was ordered into battle and, before it arrived at the front, a long grey line of armed men "crawled unperceived through the thick high canes" on the right and sent forth a "murderous volley" raking the forward units in that vicinity. Bradley's battery retreated to the rear with nine of his men dead or disabled on the ground. Colonel Bissell ordered his men to "Fall back" and the 25th Connecticut right wing retreated in confusion and disorder.[36]

The 159th New York Regiment had lost its Colonel Edward Molineaux when he was shot in the mouth by a musket ball when he rose to lead a charge. This regiment was also caught in the Rebel crossfire and suffered the same fate as the 25th Connecticut. The New Yorkers' ammunition was almost expended and they were forced to retreat to the edge of the road. Casualties of this regiment alone were 115 in dead and wounded out of the 375 who were engaged in the battle.[37]

Dwight reported that as he moved toward the front he was embarrassed when he saw the two regiments retreating in disorder and the artillery units on the right falling back. As Dwight's forces moved across the field, they outflanked the Rebels in the cane-brake, took prisoners, and then occupied the outer edge of the woods. Here Dwight was ordered to halt and hold his ground.[38]

In the meantime the troops of the 13th Connecticut Regiment, numbering around 500, and a Confederate regiment somehow outflanked each other in the woods. And now the Yanks realized that they had Rebels at their rear. A scribe for the Connecticut soldiers claimed that nearly every man in his unit began loading and firing three times a minute. The Rebels gave stubborn resistance and held their ground while the *Diana* was still sending its iron missiles into the blue line.[39]

The Yankee regiment did succeed in getting back to the field and was then ordered to fall back in line and wait for additional supporting units which Grover had ordered to the front. According to the 13th Connecticut report, its regiment had captured two caissons, one limber, four artillery horses, swords, muskets, and a great quantity of ammunition. Mention was also made that a "large and elegantly embroided silk flag," was captured, "bearing the inscription 'The Ladies of Franklin to the St. Mary Cannoneers.' " It was also stated that the trophy had at last found its way to the archives of the State of Connecticut.[40]

(Author's note: This is the same flag which was presented by Miss Louise McKerall as was noted in the first chapter of this book. According to an article in the historical issue of the *St. Mary Banner and Franklin Tribune,* dated April 28, 1959, the St. Mary Cannoneers' flag was discovered in New Orleans, by Reverend Jerry Tompkins who was the Presbyterian minister in Franklin at the time. Reverend Tompkins found the flag in the possession of the Louisiana Historical Association located in the vicinity of Lee Circle and Camp Street. It had been sent to the south sometime after the war. Reverend Tompkins led a civic group in making an appeal that the flag be returned to Franklin. Their efforts were successful and the flag though somewhat deteriorated and discolored is now exhibited in the old Grevemberg house in Franklin which was converted into a museum.)

Taylor was saddened that Colonel Reily was mortally

wounded. The Colonel received the fatal wound just before the gallant Rebel charge and he died on the field. Adding to Taylor's sorrow was the news that three more officers were wounded in the thick of battle. They were: Colonel Vincent who was shot in the neck, Adjutant J. A. Prudhomme of the Second Louisiana Cavalry and Captain R. H. Bradford.[41]

After Taylor was satisfied that the Yankee drive at Irish Bend had been checked, he ordered General Mouton to replace him and then hastened to Franklin to personally direct the train and troops which were withdrawing from Bisland. Taylor pressed his men and supplies via the Harding cut-off road eluding both fronts of the Union command who were rejoicing in the thought that Taylor and company were trapped.

Colonel Green with the rear guard composed of his own regiment, Waller's battalion, and the rifle section of Semmes battery, left the line at Bisland before daybreak, managing at the same time to move store and equipment ahead on the road to Franklin. A 24-pounder siege gun and a 12-pounder howitzer, which was disabled during Monday's action, were necessarily abandoned. Taylor reported that Colonel Green retired slowly with great coolness and steadiness before the heavy advance guard of the enemy.[42]

According to Lieutenant John West, who was in command of the rifle section of the C. S. Light Artillery and attached to Green's rear guard, an orderly retreat ensued. He stated that when his unit reached Centerville he was ordered to check the advance of the enemy. West masked his pieces while Colonel Green deployed his cavalry and when the enemy came within close range, it was fired upon by the Confederates, causing the Yanks to retreat through the town behind the cover of their artillery.[43] Tactics such as this played a great part in delaying the invaders and allowed the Confederate troops and supplies to funnel their way safely into Franklin and out on the escape road to Baldwin, Jeanerette and other points to the northwest.

Taylor saw "the handwriting on the wall," for he knew

that his troops were outpowered and outnumbered and was desperately at work trying to coordinate an orderly retreat. When the last of the Confederate troops, which were stationed at Bisland, had crossed the Bayou Yokely, they were ordered by General Sibley to set fire to the bridge. Sibley assumed that the troops at Irish Bend had already withdrawn.[44]

Mouton held the enemy at bay on the Irish Bend front until about noon when one of his staff officers, Major R. W. Sanders, who was assistant quartermaster, informed him that the troops from the lower front had retired and that the enemy was approaching Franklin. Captain Semmes of the *Diana* covered Mouton's withdrawal as the general found a by-path and succeeded in eluding his pursuers. When Mouton and his forces reached the Yokely Bridge it was almost consumed by fire but all the men crossed safely —and in the nick of time.[45]

After Mouton's forces had cleared the Irish Bend area the brave and heroic Captain Semmes withdrew the *Diana* to the docks at Franklin. There he had his crew to set fire to the magazine and the famous gunboat was "blown to atoms." The captain and crew were captured by the cavalry of the 114th New York Volunteers.[46]

The Confederates were determined not to leave anything for the Yankees, as they scuttled a number of boats in the Teche at Franklin. These included three transports, *Newsboy,* the *Gossamer,* and *Era No. 2,* all of which had been used in the transfer of troops and supplies. The Rebels also applied the match to *The Blue Hammock, Darby, Louise, Uncle Tommy,* and the *Cricket.* The *Cornie,* a hospital boat which was loaded with the Rebel sick and wounded, was transferred over to the Union command. A large supply of ammunition and army stores were also destroyed by Taylor as he fled before the Union forces who ran into each other at Franklin.[47]

When the confused pursuers tracked the Rebels to the Bayou Yokely they were frustrated even more to learn that the bridge was impassable and that Taylor had eluded them completely.[48]

About two o'clock in the afternoon Banks arrived to assess the situation. Seeing that the bridge could not be made passable before morning, and that nothing was to be gained by marching his tired troops over the long round about route of the bayou road, the general decided to go into bivouac early in the afternoon and to cover the northern approaches to the town. Grover occupied the Irish Bend battlefield, Emory held the bayou road between Grover and Franklin, and Weitzel the cut-off road.[49]

Colonel David Hunter Strother, who was a member of Banks' staff, recorded in his diary that Franklin was a town of three thousand inhabitants and many rurally beautiful residences. He mentioned that the people of the area were appalled and were utterly astounded that their troops had been beaten. The staff headquarters was established at the house of a Mr. Pierret (sic), the family having fled to escape the impending battle.[50]

Most of Taylor's men bivouacked that night in the Jeanerette area located about 15 miles above Franklin while Mouton collected his widespread troops and encamped on the plantation of Louis Grevemberg just below Jeanerette. The plantation home is now known as Albania.[51]

According to the author's knowledge the losses of the Confederates at Irish Bend and Bisland, have never been reported but are believed to be considerably less than those inflicted upon the enemy. The Union's Bisland losses were recorded as 3 officers and 37 men killed; 8 officers and 176 men wounded; all totaling 224 casualties.[52] Grover's troops at Irish Bend suffered the losses of 6 officers and 43 men killed; 17 officers and 257 men wounded; 30 men missing; in all 353 casualties.[53]

At about 5:00 a.m., while Grover was preoccupied with landing his forces at McWilliams' plantation, an important naval engagement was developing. The gunboat flotilla under Captain Cooke was alerted to some lights that were spotted across Grand Lake to the north. The lookout aboard the *Calhoun* reported the lights were on steamers headed in their direction. At daybreak the boats were recognized as the ram *Queen of the West* and the transports

Grand Duke and *Mary T*. The transports were laden with Confederate troops and the same heroic Captain Fuller of gunboat *Cotton* fame was aboard *The Queen* and in command of the little fleet.[54]

Cooke, who had already detached the *Clifton* on a mission as previously reported, immediately got the *Estrella, Calhoun* and *Arizona* underway. He ordered the gunboat to fire at long range and then arranged the boats in a crescent formation gradually closing in on the *Queen*. It wasn't long, however, before the Union gunners found their mark.

According to a diary written by acting third assistant engineer George Baird, who was aboard the *Calhoun,* Captain Fuller was quoted as saying "There is that damned *Calhoun*—I would rather see the devil than see that boat." Baird reported that as soon "as the 30-pounder Parrot would bear, it was fired at extreme elevation, for the vessels were nearly 3 miles away." Two observers aboard the *Calhoun* said they saw a shot as it left one of their guns, traced its projectory and saw it strike the *Queen*. There was an explosion followed by a rush of steam. Baird described the *Queen* as being armored around her machinery like the *Diana,* cotton clad above, but was much larger than the *Diana* affording more room in the casemate for her larger guns. But the *Queen* had no armor on her upper deck. Baird claimed that the shell fired from the *Calhoun* was a percussion shell and that it struck the roof, exploded, cut a steam pipe and set fire to the cotton.[55] The engineers were driven from the casemate and no pump could be started. In a few moments the *Queen* was ablaze and 26 of her crew were scalded or burned to death. Cooke then ceased firing, lowered all boats and rescued 90 members of the *Queen* including Captain Fuller. About 7:40 a.m. the magazine exploded and the *Queen* was no more. When the *Queen* was first ignited, her steamer consorts turned around and sped back up Chicot Pass, and then on to Butte-à-la-Rose. It was reported that Captain Fuller was taken prisoner and sent to Johnson Island where he died.

The Union gunboats, enjoying the superiority of the Atchafalaya Basin, returned to Brashear City, and later headed up towards the Teche. During this tour of duty a telegraph cable was stretched across Berwick Bay, giving the Yankees direct communication for their forces west of the Atchafalaya River to the city of New Orleans.[56]

CHAPTER IX

THE AFTERMATH

Banks' campaign of the battles of Irish Bend and Bisland was a failure due to the fact that Taylor's forces and equipment sprang loose from a carefully planned trap which involved three Union divisions, a powerful gunboat flotilla, special landing equipment, and a great amount of ammunition and food supplies. It was not only costly in materials for the invaders but the apparent great loss in lives was the big black mark against the strategy of the Union command.

According to Union diaries and regimental histories, many of the officers and men felt that Grover had "goofed" at Irish Bend. There were insinuations that Grover after landing should have directed his troops to Baldwin where he could have "bottled up" Taylor's forces. It was later rumored around the Franklin area that Madame Porter was a Yankee sympathizer, that she entertained Union officers and also that she tried to persuade Grover to take the Baldwin leg of "the horseshoe."[1]

Adding weight to this rumor was the fact that her mansion was not pillaged or burned, was constantly protected by Union troops, and that her plantation was left pretty much intact. And too, there is documented evidence from Homer Sprague's *History of the 13th Regiment of Connecticut Volunteers* relating that Madame Porter's son was released not long after he had been captured.[2]

However, the late John Caffery, who was a sugar planter and historian, mentioned the Porter-Grover rumor in an article which was published in 1959. Caffery wrote that when Grover was questioned about Madame Porter's attempt to direct him to Baldwin, he denied that any such conversation ever took place.[3]

Perhaps we'll never learn the real truth about what actually transpired. The main characters have long expired and although we have done our best to piece together some of the facts, we still find ourselves in doubt. We feel, however, that Madame Porter did take the loyalty oath to protect all of her precious possessions. It is indeed a tempting choice for one faced with similar circumstances.

An example of what could happen to a plantation owner who was not cooperative with the Union command was recorded by Homer Sprague while his regiment was stationed in the vicinity of Irish Bend.

He wrote: "A Rebel planter requested Colonel Birge to furnish a guard to protect his property. 'Certainly,' said the Colonel, 'if you are a loyal citizen of the United States.' 'I'm a loyal citizen of the Confederate States,' he answered with an oath. 'Then I can't furnish a guard,' was the rejoiner. In a few minutes, we saw, on looking back, a dense mass of smoke ascending from the dwelling; a sight far too common in Louisiana."[4]

Sprague also mentioned that they had passed the residence of a wealthy Negro, who was an extensive slave-owner, and who had raised and equipped at his own expense a company of white soldiers for the Confederate service. "His wife, it was said, was a white woman, who had come South to teach. How often the sublime topples over into the ridiculous."

Following the engagement at Irish Bend the battleground was described as a gory, bloody mess. There were so many amputations by the surgeons at the makeshift sugarhouse hospital that a large pile of legs, arms, feet and hands had developed.[5] Hosmer made these observations:

> "Toward night I go down the cart-path to the actual field, and see the broken muskets, the scattered knapsacks and clothing, the furrows where the enemy lay, the bloody pools where the dying fainted, the burial parties, the piles of corpses lying by the trenches just ready to receive them. They report that we lost in the neighborhood of four hundred and only one brigade was engaged. It was a bloody strife opposite. Leaving a party to bury the dead, we march off, and encamp in a broad field sloping down to the Teche. Permission was given to get from the neighboring plantations what was needed in the way of food; and after an exciting day the regiment was soon at rest—the rest we had won by the hardships of the three or four previous nights. Our little battle is known among the men as that of Irish Bend, by others as Indian Ridge. It does not make much of a figure in history. Newspaper reporters were not on hand; but it was sharp, obstinate and bloody."[6]

(Author's note: The preceeding quotation substantiates a story which was related by M. C. Rose of Franklin. Rose claimed that when he was a small boy his grandfather pointed across the bayou from the old Rose plantation home and described the location of a trench which was dug "two furrows wide wherein the bodies of dead soldiers were buried side by side.")

One indication of the fury of battle was that the fence which was used as a protective shield by the Rebels was almost cut to pieces by Union gunfire. The ground was literally covered with shot, shell, grape, cannister and over forty dead horses. An iron foundry and a large saw mill in the Franklin area were destroyed by the bulldozing Yankee machine.[7]

Although Taylor appeared cheerful as he beat a hasty retreat across central Louisiana remarking that he escaped without losing a "pot or a pan," he was in reality bitterly disappointed. During the course of the withdrawal operations there were a number of incidents that irritated Taylor to no end. He was frustrated with Brigadier General Sibley's actions claiming that Sibley dispatched one of his staff officers to Colonel Green with an order to fall back at once to Franklin before the enemy took possession of the cut-off road—an order which was not cleared through Taylor. Obeying Sibley's order Green immediately fell back on the Harding road and set fire to the bridge over the Bayou Yokely, taking for granted that all troops had passed. When Mouton retired with his command the bridge was still burning. Taylor was also concerned about the fate of Captain Semmes and his crew who were to use the bridge for their escape.[8]

Another incident which incensed the general was that the steamer *Cornie* laden with Confederate sick and wounded from Camp Bisland was ordered into the enemy lines under a hospital flag by General Sibley. But Taylor unaware of Sibley's action had devised a different plan. He had made arrangements to transfer the sick and wounded by means of a sufficient number of ambulances and other vehicles at the docks in Franklin.

Taylor was also miffed at Sibley for not carrying out his order to march at the head of the column to prevent straggling, select a suitable camp for the troops and wagons and then report to Taylor the selection of the camping ground for the night. Taylor claimed that Sibley did not comply with his order and that instead of being with his command he had taken a different road than his troops. Taylor also inferred that the men were straggling without order over the whole line of march and adjacent country. Taylor had Sibley report to him for an explanation to which Sibley replied that he was sick.[9]

Taylor reported that nearly all of Lieutenant Colonel Fournet's Yellow Jacket battalion, passing through the country in which the men had lived, deserted their arms and remained at their homes.

(Author's note: Although Taylor had Sibley court-martialed on several counts of disobedience of orders and unofficer-like conduct Sibley was found not guilty on all charges and set free.)[10]

As for Fournet's Yellow Jackets, the author in his research found the regiment to be a bold, fighting unit which was dedicated to the Confederate cause. Because many left the ranks while passing their homes was understandable. They were concerned about the loved ones who were left unprotected from plantation uprisings, sickness, starvation, destruction and the other vicious elements brought about by war. It was also learned that other Confederates (presumed to be Texans) broke ranks and headed for Texas. Orders were given that an effort be made to head off these deserters at Niblett's Bluff.)[11]

General Mouton, however, gave Taylor full credit for the safe withdrawal of troops from the Franklin area. He wrote,

> "It is due to the truth of history that I should here record the fact that the salvation of our retiring army was entirely owing to the bold and determined attack of our troops under the immediate command of Major General Taylor, leading the van upon the enemy at early dawn, thereby arresting the advance of the whole force of the enemy, 8,000 to 10,000 strong, with not over 1,200 men, until our retreating forces had gotten far on the road leading to the Cypremort and beyond the reach of pursuit."[12]

Now that the pressure of full scale combat had somewhat subsided, hordes of soldiers of the 19th Army Corps began stepping up the unsavory practice of foraging and confiscating. They had the convenience of being in the midst of the "land of plenty" and they couldn't resist the temptation.[13]

Pigs, chickens, beeves, sheep, vegetables, etc. were constantly being gathered and "gobbled up" by the wild-eyed army. Not being satisfied with this phase of foraging, the soldiers began breaking into homes confiscating wines, li-

From *Harper's Weekly*

FORAGING IN LOUISIANA

quors, preserves, salt meat, etc. Then the situation became ridiculous as the army of occupation transformed into an army of sackers and plunderers.

Although severe punishment was imposed on those soldiers who were found guilty of wanton destructiveness, there was no apparent slow down in these abusive tactics. The breaking of mirrors, pianos and other costly furniture was a common occurrence. A Federal scribe reported that "men of such reckless dispositions are frequently guilty of the most horrible destructions, and have been seen, in one of their raids, dressed in full robes of a Catholic priest, or ornamented with the regalia of a Free Mason, while they marched through the dust with guns upon their backs."[14]

Commonly found strewn in the road as each regiment passed were books, furniture, clocks, chinaware, portraits, ladies apparel, farming utensils and every portable thing that possibly could be imagined.

All these licentious activities imposed upon the people of the bayou country a sickening, frustrating and almost unbearable situation.

Harris Beecher in his regimental history of the 114th New York Volunteers wrote:

> "The most noticeable feature of the Teche campaign was the great number of slaves and the amusing manifestations of welcome they gave to the Yankee liberators. At every plantation, the road would be lined, and the fences covered with grinning black faces—men, women and children, curtsying and bowing, singing and dancing—all attempting to express their joy at once.
>
> " 'I'se so glad to see you all!
>
> " 'Glory to de Lord, he let me see dis bressed day!'
>
> " 'Are you all Yankees? I tot you all had horns!'
>
> " 'O! You ought ter see old mars'r run when he heard you was comin'!' "

Beecher went on to relate that most of the slaves would have their bundles all ready to leave and fall in with the troops. But he pointed out that it took the most strenuous exertions to keep the army from being clogged with thousands of negroes.[15]

Early in the morning of the 15th of April, Banks took up the pursuit of the Rebels with all of his forces—some regiments proceeding by way of Irish Bend road while others took off across the Harding short-cut. Again the Union advance was retarded by Green's rear guard.[16]

The footsore Yankees then adopted the infectious practice of seizing horses from the plantations along the way and began to enjoy the luxury of riding. Even some officers adopted this easy mode of transportation but every hour the army became more and more confused. Company and regimental organizations lost their identity among the mass of horses, carts and mules.[17] Footmen and horsemen were mingled together, horses without bridles or saddles were being conducted by rope halters, and "loaded from ears to tails with chickens and turkeys." Ofttimes the road was blocked with kicking and obstinate mules and fractious horses. Beecher reported,

> "Huge plantation carts, drawn by diminutive donkeys, were loaded down with lazy soldiers. In one instance some officers were laid out at full length in a hearse, smoking their pipes, while an ugly mule and a ragged negro driver were conducting them along the road. A soldier was being drawn by a comrade, on a hand cart. Wheelbarrows even came in use. An elegant barouche, conveying some officers, with cigaretts (sic), was drawn by a novel team composed of a cow and a mule. Skeleton buggies, family carriages, doctors' sulkies, butchers' carts, daguerrean cars, and peddlers' wagons, were all brought into requisition to complete the amusing but sad picture. Verily there was a perfect mania for riding."[18]

All this presented quite a spectacle but Banks had had enough. He ordered Company "H" of the 114th New York Infantry to establish itself by the side of the road ahead of the forces and arrest every man and officer who was riding without authority. The horses and mules were then confined in an enclosure.[19]

In David Strother's diary, he mentions that after passing Baldwin they came upon "a vast prairie with fine short grass and level as a parlor carpet. Our column was marching through in grand show. Hundreds of ponies, cattle and mules were grazing around in the distance. We first saw Camp Hunter, a camp of instruction for recruits of the Confederates. A lovelier spot could not be found in the world. A hundred thousand men could be formed and marched here in turf as smooth as a billiard table. This beautiful common was in Indian Bend, some three miles from the entrance to Indian Village." (Note: Indian Village is the settlement of the Chitimacha Indians and known as Charenton.) "I rode aside to visit the reservation of the aboriginal race. They had a poor village of cabins and about a hundred inhabitants. They said they had nothing to do with the war and had not been impressed, although they were threatened with imprisonment. They seemed so glad we had come, for they could now go to the lake and fish."[20]

We might mention here that Colonel Strother was a Virginian, a noted author and illustrator who worked under the *nom de plume* of Porte Crayon. At the outbreak of the war, however, he had a difficult decision to make. After much deliberation he chose to fight for the North but it was apparent that he had great concern for the feelings of the South. Some of that concern is reflected in the following stories which were compiled by your author from Strother's diary which appeared in Cecil D. Eby's book *A Virginia Yankee in the Civil War.* Colonel Strother constantly rode and fought alongside General Weitzel. About two miles east of Jeanerette, Strother and his group stopped at the house of and old Frenchman by the name of Say (sic—probably meant Fay). The old man couldn't speak English but did manage to explain that he was distressed about an incident which involved the invaders. He complained that the neighboring house of his married daughter had been sacked even to the destruction of his granddaughter's toys. Although a guard was posted at the plantation foraging and sacking continued.

Weitzel did not condone this type of behavior and had about a hundred Yankees arrested. He then asked Strother's advice as to what he should do with the men. Strother suggested that the general should lecture the prisoners and then send them back to their regiments. Weitzel felt that perhaps this was the best way to go about it and as he spoke to the men "every fellow commenced with a rigamarole apology, one breaking in after another until the whole band were in full blast like an orchestra." When Weitzel finally got the men quieted down he recalled their offenses, their evil consequences and then dismissed them with an admonition. They gave the general three cheers, promised to whip the Rebels and "scattered like a group of excused schoolboys."

When the Yankee forces approached the town of Jeanerette, Strother received permission from Weitzel to visit his cousins, Mrs. Nancy Weeks and Miss Fanny Hunter, who were sisters. He rode ahead of Weitzel's forces, crossed a bridge at Jeanerette and headed to the home of Alfred Weeks.

There he discovered Miss Hunter on the porch with a young lady who was her neice Mary Weeks—a playmate of Strother's daughter during a bygone visit. He learned that Mrs. Weeks had given birth to a child two days before he arrived.

Mary immediately inquired about Captain O. J. Semmes of the gunboat *Diana* who was captured by the Union forces after Semmes and his crew scuttled the vessel at Franklin. She was engaged to the captain and Strother assured her that Semmes was in good health.[21]

Colonel Strother then told in his diary of the tearful reunion when he was invited into the house to see Nancy and her newborn child. "I have never seen so strong a picture of concentrated pride, anger and distress." The woman at first refused the U. S. protection, but under the circumstances decided to accept it, provided there would be no conditions.

He wrote: "Nancy wept aloud and grasped my hand convulsively. Tears gushed to my eyes and I covered my face with my hands and sobbed. Those proud, generous, fiery and loving hearts had been of my dearest and earliest friends. I soothed her to quiet and sat down beside her." But Nancy couldn't conceal her loyalty to the South and "let loose" with an emotional outburst that echoed throughout the household.

"Thank God," she exclaimed, as she looked at her child, "she was born day before yesterday while the Confederate flag still floated here."[22]

(Author's note: After a thorough research, I found that Captain Semmes, following his capture, was taken to New Orleans and delivered to the Provost Marshal at that city. Semmes was then turned over to Major J. W. Burgess of the 6th New York Regiment along with about 50 other Confederate officers and conveyed to Fortress Monroe. On June 10, 1863, Captain Semmes along with other prisoners, most of whom were officers, while being transferred from Fortress Monroe to Fort Delaware, Delaware aboard the steamer *Maple Leaf,* suddenly overpowered the guard and made their escape. Semmes, after experiencing a hazardous journey crossing the Mississippi and passing through the Yankee lines, succeeded in rejoining his command. On November 7, 1863, he was promoted to major of the Louisiana artillery and held that commission when he received his parole at Mobile on May 9, 1865, while a member of the staff of Richard Taylor. The author never was able to find out what happened between Mary Weeks and Semmes during all these years. A record reveals, however, that Semmes married Amante Gaines at Mobile, Alabama on December 17, 1873.)[23]

CHAPTER X

DESTRUCTION OF THE SALT WORKS

Taylor managed to keep his forces a safe distance ahead of his adversaries and at the same time destroy ammunition dumps, burn stockpiles of cotton, scuttle boats and do away with anything that would be of use to the enemy. While Taylor was in New Iberia, Lieutenant Joshua Humphreys, who was in command of the gunboat *Stevens,* reported that his vessel was in an unfinished condition and unfit for action. Taylor fearing that he would have a problem keeping the vessel out of reach of the Yankees ordered the *Stevens* to be sunk five miles below the city as an impediment to the ascending Federal gunboats. But the *Stevens* was only sunk two miles below New Iberia, much to Taylor's disappointment.[1]

We might mention here that the *Stevens* was the same gunboat *Hart* which had been involved earlier in the campaign.[2] The vessel was described as one of the best and fastest gunboats in the Rebel navy, carrying one 32-pound rifled cannon forward, a similar cannon aft, and two small smooth-base 24-pound brass pieces under her casement. Her machinery and bulkheads were protected by three-inch railroad iron, the heaviest kind in use. She had two "splendid" engines aboard, of twenty-inch cylinder, seven foot stroke. There were four double-flue boilers on the boat. Reconditioning and revamping of this vessel began the day after the burning of the *Cotton*. For some reason the gunboat was incapable of doing battle in spite of the fact that it had been worked on for a three month period.[3]

On the 17th of April, Major A. Power Gallway of the 173rd New York Infantry began an expedition through St. Martinville with his regiment and a section of Battery "F," 1st U. S. Artillery. He followed the road along the Teche which led to Breaux Bridge. About five miles south of this town, near the settlement of Parks, ten of Gallway's mounted men, who were scouting ahead of the troops, engaged in a skirmish with Rebel pickets and claimed to have captured two prisoners and three horses. Shortly thereafter, Gallway noticed a heavy smoke in the direction of Breaux Bridge and when he arrived in the town found the Bayou Teche bridge engulfed in flames. The major learned that there had been a Rebel force of over 500 cavalry men in the vicinity just before his arrival.[4]

Gallway was also informed that a number of steamboats had passed up the bayou the day before and were probably grounded at the intersection of Bayou Teche and Bayou Fusilier where the water depth was considered too shallow for steamboat navigation. Gallway then set out for Opelousas on April 19th and found the Confederate steamers scuttled near the forenamed intersection. The boats were identified as the *Darby, Louise, Blue Hammock,* and the *Cricket*. The *Uncle Tommy* was burned higher up in the Teche.[5] (Author's Note: These are the same boats reported earlier by another source as being scuttled near Franklin.)

Cargoes of beef, rum, sugar and commissary stores, cloth, uniforms, and large quantities of arms and ammunition were destroyed along with the boats. However the Rebels managed to take off portions of the cargoes of ammunition and arms by means of barges before firing the vessels.

Large stores of provisions and ammunition were destroy-

NEW IBERIA DURING THE CIVIL WAR

ed with these boats, including some twenty thousand pounds of bacon and nearly a thousand cases of ammunition.

But much to Gallway's chagrin he found that the bridge across Bayou Fusilier was also burned and this meant another delay. The following day, the major rounded up 50 Negroes from nearby plantations and repaired the bridge. After crossing with his command Gallway found a hospital on the left bank of the bayou with about twenty of the enemy's sick and wounded.

Gallway mentioned in his report that his forces had captured 24 prisoners not including the captain of the *Uncle Tommy*. He also wrote that he passed the charred remains of several barges in the Teche and found along the roadside large quantities of shot, new cavalry sabers, barrels of oil and around a thousand barrels of salt. On his march he seized a thousand barrels of corn and distributed them to the poorer families of the area. He gave 300 barrels to Rev. M. Bernard, curè of the parish for distribution and about 400 barrels were stored in a crib on Mr. Camean's (sic) plantation to await disposition. Gallway halted on the evening of the 20th about seven miles below Opelousas and bivouacked there for the night.[6]

The following humorous incidents occurred as the Federal forces were approaching New Iberia. While the Confederates were in the process of evacuating via the St. Martinville and Vermilionville routes, there was some display of stubbornness and wild patriotism within the ranks. Lt. Colonel I. D. Blair, who was under the influence of Louisiana rum, made it known to those around him that he was going to fight the whole Union army single-handed. Even though he was told that over 5,000 Yankees were approaching the city he still maintained he could whip them all. His regimental friends, however, became quite concerned about the welfare of the colonel and came up with a unique plan. Someone in the ranks challenged Blair to a horse race from New Iberia to St. Martinville. He accepted the offer and started out of town at a full run. This scheme saved the colonel the anguish of being captured by the enemy.[7]

Another Confederate soldier who had drunk too many toasts to the ladies that morning and who also wanted to take on the whole Union army by himself was Ed B. Talbot of Iberville parish. Talbot bravely exposed himself to the Federals who were drawn up in a line of battle of about a hundred yards in width and gradually approaching the town. As a matter of fact Talbot rode in front of the Union ranks calling them names and daring them to fight. The Federal regiments held their fire for fear of hitting the women and children who were exposed in the background.

After much difficulty, his buddies succeeded in having him fall back, telling him that he was ordered to take charge of an ambush in the rear. It was reported that Talbot lived to be one of the best lawyers and judges in the state and at the same time "setting an example of sobriety and general rectitude."[8]

General Dwight entered New Iberia on April 16th and issued a report revealing his disgust for the intolerable action of Federal troops in the area. His report included the following: "The scenes of disorder and pillage on these two days march were disgraceful to civilized war. Houses were entered and all in them destroyed in the most wanton manner. Ladies were frightened into delivering their jewels and valuables into the hands of the soldiers by threats of violence toward their husbands. Negro women were ravished in the presence of white women and children. These disgusting scenes were due to the want of discipline in the army, and to the incompetency of regimental officers." Dwight also mentioned that some of the soldiers in his brigade got ahold of Louisiana rum and caused quite a bit of noise and confusion.[9]

Captain John G. Mudge who served in the Department of the Gulf under Banks wrote the following in his diary:

> "We reached New Iberia near night after a march of some 30 miles. At this place, on the outskirts of the village, our advance had had a skirmish with the Rebs and some half a dozen of the latter lay dead by the roadside —as we marched by in the early morning to camp for

the night, at some three miles distance. The spot of the skirmish a few hours before was a beautiful plantation. The home of one of those French families, who in the past had added lustre and renown to the history of the state, and in consideration of the well-known hostility of the owners to the Union and that the Rebs had fired from this house upon our advance. The boys were allowed to go through it; sack, pillage and destroy every article within its walls. One who has never seen a house 'sacked' by 'the boys' can have no idea how faithfully they 'do their work.' "[10]

Ever since Banks took over command of the Department of the Gulf, he had harbored a strong desire to eliminate the salt works at Petite Anse Island. Colonel William B. Kimball of the 12th Maine Infantry, who was in command of the second brigade in Grover's division, was ordered to the island. He left New Iberia on the night of April 17th with his regiment, along with the 41st Massachusetts Infantry, one company from the 24th Connecticut and one section of Nims' battery. Kimball reached the island early the next morning and found that the enemy had evacuated his works and removed his guns. He then proceeded at once to destroy all the buildings, 18 in number, which were connected with the salt works. The destruction included steam-engines, windlasses, boilers, mining implements, miscellaneous machinery, and 600 barrels of salt which were ready for shipment. He blew up the "bomb-proof" magazine which was connected with the fortification on the island and the salt works was destroyed.[11]

Colonel Kimball transported a ton of powder and about a ton of nails to New Iberia and turned it over to Captain Alanson B. Long who was provost marshal at that place.[12] It was also reported that a large number of horses were captured in the operation.[13]

(Author's note: Evidentally the Federal command had blundered in destroying the salt works, because it was not long afterwards that a special study was authorized for possible utilization of the mine. Samuel Hotaling conducted the study and a Dr. J. L. Riddell, who was a chemist at New Orleans, made the salt analysis. We quote the following excerpts from Hotaling's report.

> "This small town (New Iberia) is most beautifully situated in the midst of an extended level plain of the most productive farming land, and is elevated about ten feet (as is all the land on the Teche) above the line of the bayou. This town has one main business street running rather crookedly parallel to the bayou, with all its other streets crossing each other at right angles, and extending over the plain far as the eye could well reach giving evidence of a most extensive site for a much larger and more business town that now exists there. Before this most treasonable rebellion it was a most thriving business place.[14]
>
> "About six o'clock in the morning (around the 10th of May) we left the town and travelled in a SSW direction over a most beautiful level prairie plain about six miles distant. This plain is so very much of a dead level, that the land, although a very rich soil, is deemed by the farmers about valueless, because the water falling upon it finds no declivity by which to run off from its very flat even surface. We approached the celebrated raised plank road, which was built through a sea swamp, about two miles through the swamp to the island of Petite Anse. This road is the only land passage to the island, and is so narrow that the teams or vehicles can not pass each other upon it. A sign post at either end designates the hours of the day for passing either way along the road. By this crossing way we reached the northeasterly border of the island, and then by a winding road over its undulating, yet cultivating, surface, a distance of about two miles to its most southerly border, we approached the great salt Eldorado of North America.[15]
>
> "I was informed that from 400 to 600 men were constantly employed during a portion of last year, a part of the time both day and night, to exhume and bar-

rel the salt and load it up on from 100 to 500 teams, constantly there on the ground and driven from almost every section of the Confederate slave states, each teamster standing about and in most anxious waiting, with cash in hand, the next turn for their most wished for load.

"I have been assured by persons who knew the facts that Judge Avery has received within the past year, over $1,200,000 for this salt in addition to the many other smaller sums which have been received during the same time by the other contracting parties at the mine. It is said there has been received in all at the works for this salt within the last fiscal year the enormous sum of from two to three million dollars. Such another prolific source of money making has never yet been discovered within the United States since the formation of our government.

"All of these buildings and the machinery works have been entirely destroyed by our Union army. Nothing remains but one or two frail sheds, the lining of the pits and several small stocks of salt blocks piled around upon the earth near the walls. I am assured by Major General Banks that the Confederate guns were loaded with the salt and fired upon our soldiers."[16]

Generals and other top ranking officials always managed to set up their headquarters in the finest homes during time of war. When the Federal troops moved into New Iberia this proved to be no exception for Banks took over the beautiful old Weeks mansion—now known as the famous "Shadows on the Teche."[17]

After David Weeks, the builder of "The Shadows," had expired, his widow married Judge John Moore, and she was living in the home at the time of the Yankee occupation. General Banks, arranging the household so that he would not be disturbed, had Mrs. Moore occupy the upper portion of the building, while the general and his staff utilized the lower floor.

It was reported that the flower gardens were unavoidably destroyed, a Federal flag floated over the front entrance of the grounds, and that a guard stood nearby.

An incident which happened at this time involved two young southern ladies who were paying a visit to their old friend, Mrs. Moore. Misses Lelia and Mary Robertson while entering the front gate stoutly refused to salute the colors. This was considered an act of rebellion according to the then prevailing military rules. They were called in before the general who dealt with them quite firmly. After much discussion and several conferences, the two young ladies were freed. It was reported that Mrs. Moore died at "The Shadows" during the war.[18]

Companies "A," "E," "F," and "G" of the 52nd Massachusetts Regiment were detailed by the Federal command to remain in New Iberia and hold it while the other Union forces were pressing on towards Vermilionville.[19]

J. F. Moors, chaplain of the regiment, told a story about Josiah A. Richmond of Company "E" who had a horse that didn't suit him very well. One day while the captain had his horse saddled for a ride near the town, he met a Rebel coming down the road mounted on a fine looking horse. Richmond hailed the man and said "I would like to swap horses with you."[20]

The Rebel, not expecting to make a trade nor wanting to force matters, got off his horse, removed and changed the saddles and bridles, handed the reins over to the captain, mounted his new horse and rode away. During the whole transaction not a word was spoken. The captain noticed a sort of vicious smile on the face of the Reb as he rode away, but thought little of it at the time, but afterwards had occasion to recall it.

Although Captain Richmond's conscience troubled him for taking the horse away from the man, he nevertheless felt quite proud of his new acquisition. The captain then mounted his new horse and rode out into the country. It didn't take him long, however, to find out that he didn't have such a pious horse, but one like "Josh Billings' mule, of which he said that if he was going to break him, he would begin at the forward end."

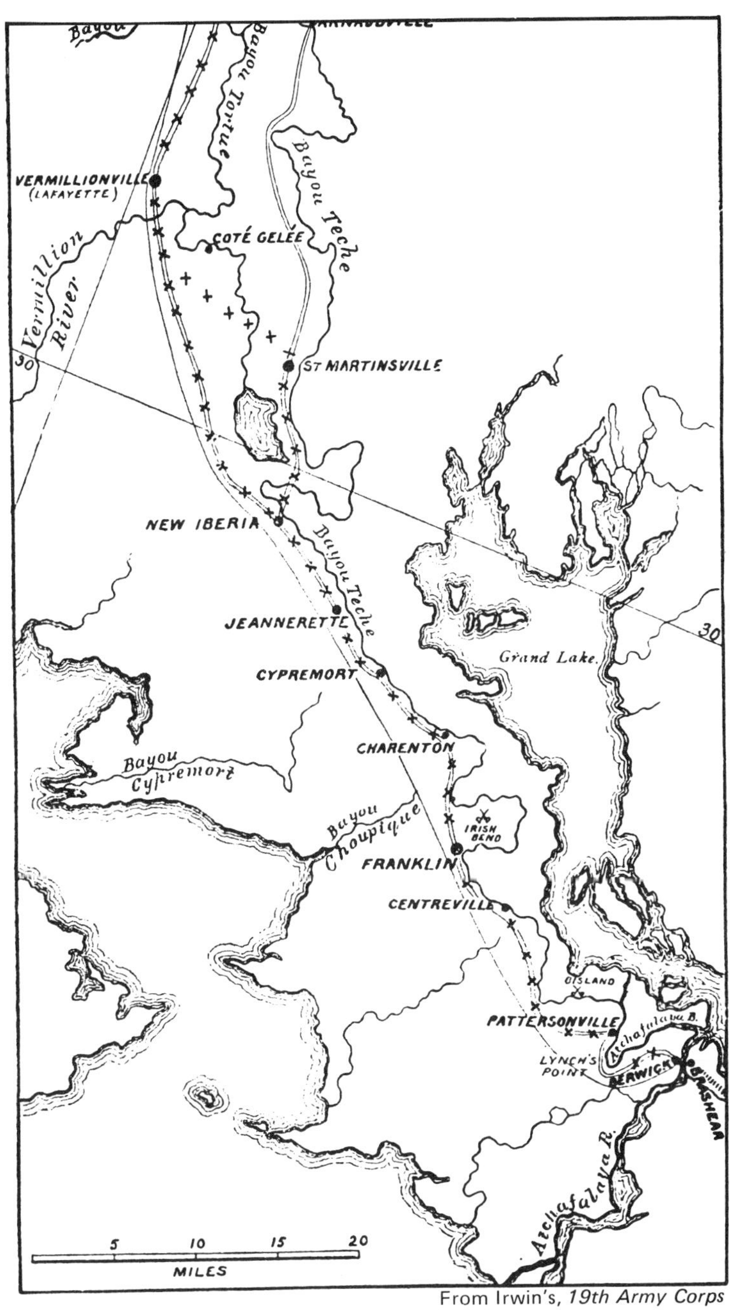

From Irwin's, *19th Army Corps*

MAP OF TECHE AND GRAND LAKE AREA

The next day while Richmond and Captain George Bliss of Company "G" were riding towards Bayou Petite Anse at the salt works to shoot alligators, Richmond's horse began to get out of hand. After a series of plunges and bolts, the horse succeeded in throwing the captain in a ditch where he remained unconscious for a few moments. The horse then took off across the plain and the captain never saw him again and never wanted to. Captain Richmond recalled many times that "sardonic smile" on the face of the Rebel when the horses were exchanged. Chaplain Moors concluded that this was one Rebel horse that thought he had contributed to the Confederate cause by killing one Yank.[21]

While in New Iberia the Union forces took over a large foundry which was used in manufacturing cannons, munitions of war, gun carriages, etc. They also seized a large sawmill.[22]

A medical detachment from the 130th Illinois converted a church into a hospital. The pews were taken out and replaced with cots. (This is believed to be the Episcopal church which still stands on Main Street in New Iberia.)[23]

A complete press was found and taken over by members of the same regiment. The men found some old pieces of wallpaper in an abandoned store and published on the blank side a new periodical which was called "Unconditional Surrender—Grant."

Still nestled among ancient oaks and magnolias is Dulcito, the stately mansion, located about five miles west of New Iberia, which played an important role in the Teche campaign. The big beautiful home, which overlooks "Lake Tasse" (now known as Spanish Lake), was mustered into service by the Confederates as a temporary field hospital for wounded soldiers. The unique water well, said to be the deepest in the area, evidentally accommodated the soldiers from nearby Camp Pratt which was spread out over a wide area. It was reported that when the Union forces occupied the general area they used the facilities of this plantation for their own conveniences. The home is now owned by the Trappey family of New Iberia.[24]

Another prominent plantation in the area which was used during the War between the States was Belmont, located about four miles north of New Iberia in the direction of St. Martinville. Banks and his cavalry took over the premises which served as a base for their operations, using the beautiful Belmont mansion as headquarters. The Union troops broke up the fencing for firewood, tore down some of the slave quarters and attempted to destroy the house. They also removed the rosewood grand piano from the house, took off the strings and used it for a horse trough to feed and water their horses.[25] (Author's note: Many of the slaves on this plantation remained loyal, one of whom, by the name of Harry Mahoney, was later elected to the Louisiana Legislature. Mahoney was taught by Mary Peebles Wyche, the wife of Major John Fletcher Wyche, owner of Belmont. It was reported that Mahoney was the last Negro to leave the legislature and one of the first to be elected to it. A wagon train which originated in Franklin picked up some families along the way and wound up in Jasper, Texas out of the clutches of the invading army. Mrs. Wyche, with her son James and several slaves, joined the train and did not return until 1865. Mrs. Wyche paid off the back taxes in gold which she had smuggled in her undergarments and money which she had earned from growing two cotton crops in Texas. The beautiful mansion was destroyed by fire in 1947 and the home now standing is a replica of the original. Mr. and Mrs. James Wyche, Jr., are the present owners of the historic plantation.)

During this period of Yankee occupation, Negroes in St. Martinville, under the leadership of mulattoes, organized an uprising against the whites. The insurgents felt that, since practically all of the able-bodied whites were occupied on fronts outside the area, the capture of the town would be an easy undertaking. A detachment of Federal soldiers, who were stationed in St. Martinville, heard about the armed uprising and threats of disaster. They promptly went to the aid of the white citizens and were joined by Captain Stone of Company "F," 52nd Massachusetts Regiment, with his squad of 30 men.[26]

The Federal units and some armed citizens took their positions near the west approach of the bridge, which spans the bayou, and as the Negroes attempted to cross over into town, they were ordered to halt. The Negro leaders, believing that the northern troops wouldn't fire at them, continued to advance. Then the troops and citizens opened fire and after a sharp skirmish, in which the whites gained the advantage, the Negroes broke out in a running retreat.

A chase ensued in which a large number of Negroes were shot. The mulatto leader and nine others who were involved in the uprising were captured and brought to the bridge. Their arms and legs were pinioned, nooses placed around their necks, and at a given signal they were strung up and left dangling in the air. At night, the friends of the victims came and carried their bodies away. With the trouble over, Captain Stone and his unit returned to New Iberia.[27]

CHAPTER XI

THE BATTLE OF VERMILION BRIDGE

Although Taylor's main troops were a safe distance ahead of Banks' invaders, the Confederate wagon train was somewhat slower in its process of retreating and consequently trailed in the rear of the north-bound column. The Federal troops which had left for Vermilionville by the St. Martinville road came to an abrupt stop as they found the Bayou Tortue bridge destroyed.[1] However, those troops which traveled the road to the west of Lake Tasse (Spanish Lake) were on a more direct route to Vermilionville and their advance units were able to catch sight of Taylor's vehicular column just before it made the crossing at Vermilion bridge. Scouts from the 6th New York Regiment, who were mounted, reported they had captured three of the wagons although they had counted thirty.[2] As soon as the last wagon crossed, Taylor set fire to the bridge and positioned his artillery and infantry around the upper approach of the bridge area in an effective line of defense. This was April 17, 1863. Taylor not only stopped the Federal forces from crossing but prevented them from repairing the bridge.

From *Campfires and Battlefields*

BATTLE OF VERMILION BAYOU

There was only one thing left for the stymied Yanks to do and that was to drive Taylor out of his position of strategic advantage. This would then enable the invaders to throw a pontoon bridge across the bayou.[3]

Captain Henry Closson, U.S.A. Chief of Artillery, advanced to the skirmish line of the Sixth and began hammering away at the enemy—a distance of about 1500 yards. He was later supported by four guns from Nims' battery. The battle of Vermilion Bridge lasted for about four hours with apparently no great loss in dead or wounded on either side. Taylor, satisfied that most of his troops and train were a safe distance ahead, picked up his wounded and moved out of range of heavy Yankee fire.

This had been a weary day for the Federal forces who had marched 20 or 30 miles over a hot, dusty trail, trying desperately to catch up with the Rebels and now they welcomed the chance to rest on the high banks overlooking the Vermilion. The following day, while awaiting the construction of the new bridge, nearly half the Yankee force decided to take advantage of the opportunity by stripping and bathing in the bayou.[4]

Suddenly without an instant's warning, a troop of Taylor's cavalry dashed down the opposite bank and opened fire on the naked men. This is how one observer described the scene:

> "Such a spectacle never before was seen. The long roll was sounding and naked men, in every direction, were making a dash for their guns, trying to dress as they ran. Some with their trousers on hind side before; didn't know whether they were advancing or retreating, and some ran the wrong way, others, with simply a shirt and cap, were trying to adjust their belts. Officers were swearing and mounted aids were dashing about, trying to make order out of confusion."[5]

Taylor resumed his retreat at noon, April 17th, while the Feds were still obsessed with the problem of crossing the bayou. The Confederate forces, which were now well rested, passed through Opelousas and Washington on the 18th and

19th. Colonel Green's rear guard cavalry maintained its effective role of retarding and frustrating the Yankee operations. On the following day Taylor found himself with all his trains behind the Bayous Cocodrie and Boeuf.[6]

On the 20th Mouton was ordered with all the cavalry, except Waller's battalion, westward to Niblett's Bluff, on the Sabine River. Then Taylor along with Waller and the column of worn infantrymen continued their steady retreat towards Alexandria halting the main force at Lecompte. Again Taylor used his most effective defensive tactic—he burned the bridges at the Cocodrie and Boeuf.[7]

On the morning of April 19th, General Banks, satisfied that the pontoon bridge across the Vermilion had been constructed, took off again after Taylor.[8] The village of Vermilionville, now known as Lafayette, was described as being a town of some three hundred inhabitants, with two churches and a convent as its principle buildings.[9]

One thing which was soon apparent to the Yankees was that the name Mouton represented important leaders of the community. On entering the village the soldiers passed the elegant residence of ex-Governor Alexander Mouton who was the president of the convention which caused the secession of the state. Nearby stood the home of the brave General Mouton who combined his strategic talents with those of Taylor in executing the amazing withdrawal from the Franklin area.[10] From almost every house the people hung towels, pillow cases and handkerchiefs as flags of truce.[11]

After marching through the town and entering the agricultural region, the infantrymen began to enjoy the panorama of snow-white fields of unpicked cotton, a novel sight for any Yankee. About two miles beyond the village the 114th New York turned off the road during the heat of the day and sought shelter at a deserted mansion which belonged to a wealthy man who also bore the name of Mouton.[12]

After dinner the men strolled around the grounds and then went in to examine the contents of the house. They found Brussels carpets, mosaic floors, frescoed halls, chinaware, mirrors, solid mahogany furniture and an extensive library. They were "astonished at the proofs of opulence and luxury which southern life afforded."

Shortly the regiment was on the road again passing through fine rolling country. But the men began to suffer from thirst and through desperation drank anything they could find. They even drank from sink holes where the water was described as warm and stagnant.

Again the acts of Banks' desolating army were recorded. Fences were torn down and burned, houses rifled, fields trampled over, and carcasses of butchered cattle were commonplace.[13] The stubborn Federal forces continued their northerly trek toward Opelousas in a driving rain, marching through water and mud, while Taylor was many miles away enjoying his free position.[14]

However, there was one segment of Taylor's responsibility which was in big trouble and that was Fort Burton at Butte-à-la-Rose. Due to the widespread withdrawal operations of the Confederate forces, the deep basin fortification became isolated from its main forces—and there was hardly anything that Taylor could do to save it.

The fort was protected by two siege guns (a 24- and 32-pounder), a garrison of about 60 men under the command of Captain Holmes of the Crescent Regiment, the gunboats *Mary T* and *Grand Duke* (which had accompanied the ill-fated *Queen of the West* in the Grand Lake encounter), and a large quantity of ammunition and commissary stores.[15]

The *Mary T* had been "fitted up" into a Southern war vessel carrying two 24-pounders, two light 12-pounders, a small howitzer, and a company of sharpshooters. The name of the *Mary T,* however, was changed to the *Cotton* in honor of Captain Fuller's famous old boat which had been sunk in Bayou Teche during January.

Lt. Commander Cooke, aboard the *U.S.S. Estrella* and commanding the gunboat fleet which included the *Clifton, Arizona* and *Calhoun* set out to attack and capture the strategic Butte-à-la-Rose fortification. The four gunboats proceeded up Bayou Chene and the Atchafalaya River and on the 19th of April, 1863, Cooke sent the *Arizona,* under Captain Upton, on ahead to reconnoiter the place. Contrabands had already warned the Yankees that sharpshooters at the fort had been undergoing strenuous target practicing and would be a tough force to subdue.[16]

The following day all Federal gunboats attacked and a sharp battle ensued. The *Calhoun* and *Clifton* were struck several times, while the latter had the stub end of one air pump link shot away, but fortunately for the crew the other air pump carried the load.

The firing became so hot that the overpowered Confederate gunboats left the scene of action. Assistant Engineer Baird, aboard the *Calhoun,* reported that they had no small boats to make a landing at the fortress because their boats were crushed by trees as the gunboats squeezed their way through the narrow bayou approaches. Baird mentioned, however, that while his vessel was in pursuit of the *Grand Duke,* one of the gunners got off a lucky shot which tore off the stern boom of the Rebel steamer and the crew of the *Calhoun* immediately seized the small boat which fell into the water.[17]

This boat was the one used in landing at the fort and capturing the "Louisiana Tigers" who found it impossible to escape.

As soon as Federal transports arrived, 800 soldiers from the 16th New Hampshire Regiment were landed at the butte which could only accommodate about 70 men. Baird explained that the Rebels had felled cypress trees and moss in developing a walkable area in the swamp behind the fort. It was pointed out that the main purpose of the tree slashing was to secure a clear view in case of Federal attack from that direction. The Union commander took advantage of the situation by ordering the excess soldiers to occupy the matted area.

The captured soldiers were described as well dressed, neat, polite, and educated young men. The *Estrella* took the prisoners back to Brashear City.[18]

Taking Butte-à-la-Rose gave the Federal command complete control of the Atchafalaya and at the same time opened communications by way of Port Barre on the Courtableau. Cooke then hastened up the Atchafalaya to make his report to Farragut who was stationed in the Mississippi near the mouth of Red River.[19]

(Author's note: A Confederate court martial was held in Shreveport at a later date trying Captain Alexander Grant of the *Mary T* for disobedience of orders. According to the charge, Captain Grant was ordered repeatedly by Captain Holmes, who was in command of the fort, to stand-by and assist the garrison in its needs. Captain Holmes charged that the *Mary T* abandoned the fort and the garrison without making proper efforts to assist in the defense or in the removal of the garrison guns and stores. Grant pleaded "not guilty" and the court "after mature deliberation on the testimony adduced" found the accused "not guilty." Captain Grant was then acquitted of the charge.)[20]

After a miserable march which included the fording of several bridgeless streams, the Yankees approached the town of Opelousas. The troops then closed ranks and made their entree in fine style with the bands playing the unwelcome strains of "Yankee Doodle." The town was described as being of considerable beauty, having three churches, a nunnery and a population of between fifteen hundred and two thousand people. The Rebel state government was careful to move again before the Union army entered and, as one Yankee remarked, "the Louisiana state capitol was now on wheels." What made the acquisition of Opelousas so interesting to General Banks was the fact that it was in the heart of the great cotton producing region to which he had long been aiming to get access.[21]

James Hosmer gave the following account of a tour which was taken of the "Swayze Place" at Opelousas:

> "We made our way through a forest (killing a rattlesnake in our course), entered the plantation gate, passed through a rather squalid purlieu of negro huts, then came to the mansion itself,—a one-story dwelling, with neat veranda and some marks of taste, though house and surroundings lacked finish. The garden was a wreck;

and through we passed without hinderance, by the open door, into what had been elegantly furnished apartments. One had been a library; and the floor was strewn with a litter of valuable books. One had been a dining-room, at one side of which stood a handsomely carved sideboard. In the parlor was a rich piano, and other furniture in keeping,—all overturned, scattered, and marred.

"We went into bedrooms, where were handsome canopied beds, and heavy furniture of rosewood. In one was a large mirror, in which I caught sight of a very swarthy and travel-stained warrior, whom I should never have recognized. I hurried out with an uncomfortable feeling. The pillage and destruction was due in part to our soldiers, in part to the negroes. It was discreditable and painful."[22]

About six miles above Opelousas, the Federal troops crossed a large trestle bridge over a marshy flat and entered the town of Washington. One scribe reported that the place was of considerable size, much larger than Opelousas, but was squalid and dirty. He wrote, "Among the boys it afterwards went by the name of 'niggertown,' owing to its great number of black inhabitants."[23]

As the Federal units advanced to the northern edge of the town, they came upon steep banks overlooking the Bayou Courtableau. This stream was wide and navigable and the number of warehouses along the banks made it evident that Washington had once been a place of considerable business. The main bridge was burned, and after General Banks had his engineers construct a temporary bridge of flatboats, he notified the officials of the town that if he ever came back to Washington he would expect to find a new bridge at this point, otherwise he would lay the town in ashes. (Author's note: The people of the community fearing that the 19th Army Corps would return and stick to their threat, gathered white and black labor, used carts and mules, and built a new bridge.)[24]

Banks headquartered at Opelousas, learned from his

aide-de-camp that Admiral Porter was poised at the mouth of Red River with the gunboats *Benton, Lafayette, Pittsburg, Price,* the ram *Switzerland*, and the tugboat *Ivy*. With these vessels Porter had run the batteries of Vicksburg in preparation for Grant's movement. Porter also notified Banks that he would meet his army at Alexandria. On the morning of May 4th, the Union general ordered Dwight to move ahead from his advance position at Washington to be followed by Weitzel that afternoon and Emory the next morning. Emory, however, was not well and finally consented to his surgeon's advice to go to New Orleans for a brief visit.[25]

In the meantime Captain Howard Dwight, brother to the brigadier general, was killed while riding to the front to join the advance commanded by his brother. According to a Union report, the captain was surprised and cut-off at a short turn in the Bayou Boeuf road by a party of armed men on the opposite bank. Concealed from an ambulance and the few orderlies that followed, Captain Dwight found himself pretty much alone during this encounter. Armed only with a sword and seeing that escape was hopeless, he instantly declared his readiness to surrender. But the guerillas, the report continued, cried, "Surrender be damned!" and shot the captain dead.[26]

Banks was incensed when he heard this report and ordered General Dwight to arrest a hundred white men near his line of march and to send these men to New Orleans where they were to be held as hostages until the "murderers" were delivered.

There were not a hundred white men to be found in the region where Dwight was marching but many men were imprisoned and subjected to stiff punishment as the result of this harsh measure. While under a flag of truce, Dwight demanded from Taylor the surrender of his brother's "murderers." The Confederate officers not only disavowed the crime but severely condemned such an act and declared that the alleged criminals were not to be found.[27]

Taylor managed to keep his forces well out of reach of the advancing Union army and Banks, having encountered

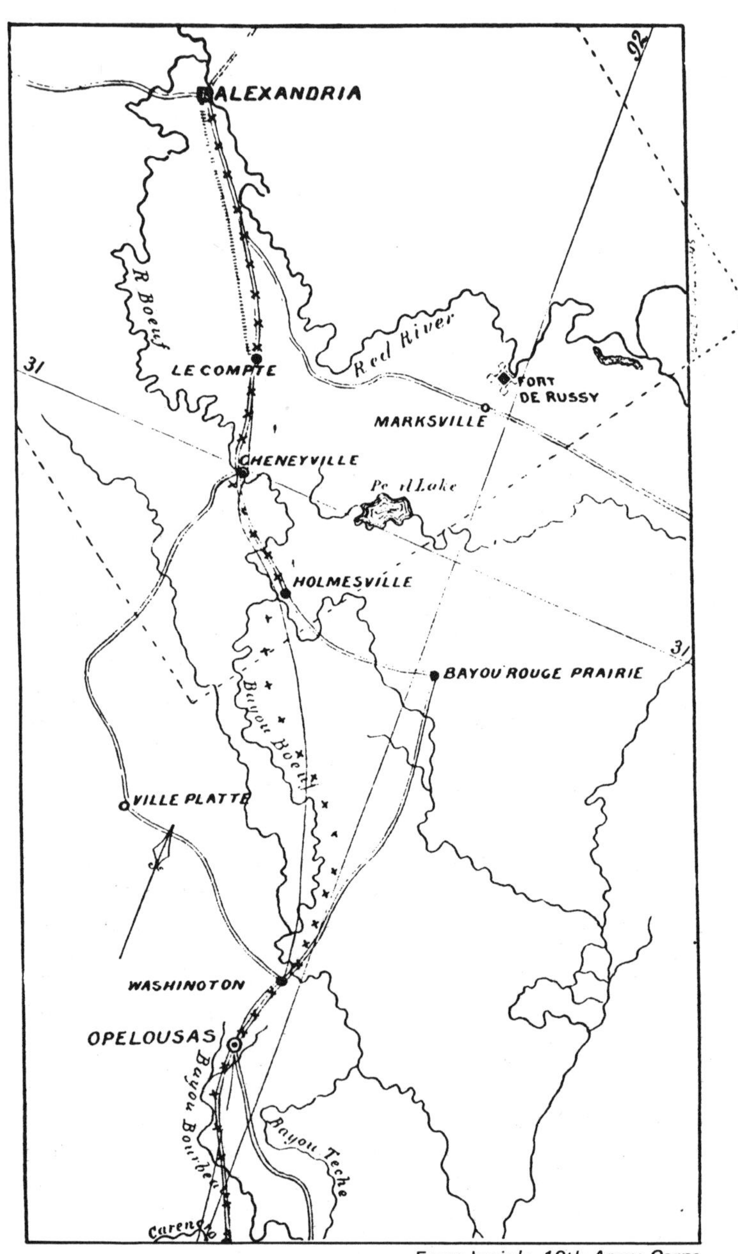

From Irwin's, *19th Army Corps*

MAP OF OPELOUSAS AND ALEXANDRIA AREA

no opposition and enjoying the good weather, made good time. He promised to meet Admiral Porter in Alexandria on the morning of May 9th but Banks' men were "hepped up" to the point where they wanted to march much faster in order to beat Porter to the city.

General Kirby Smith, who had been in command of the Trans-Mississippi Department, had been given a new and separate assignment earlier—during the month of January. He was appointed commander of the Southwestern Army, embracing the Department of West Louisiana and Texas.[28] In the latter part of April, he retired to Shreveport, two hundred miles up Red River and began to organize his administration.[29]

Fort De Russy, located east of Alexandria, on the south bank of the Red River, was the only brarrier which stood in the way of Porter's westward trek. However, the Confederate command, realizing that the fort would soon be attacked by the Federal navy and also that the rear of the fortification was open to an invasion by the Federal land forces by way of Marksville, declared Fort De Russy as being untenable and began making plans for its abandonment. Consequently, orders were issued that the fort be dismantled and the garrison withdraw to a safer location up the Red River.[30]

Although Porter had ordered up the *Estrella* and *Arizona* to "beef up" his own fleet in preparation for the Red River campaign, he experienced a setback in the vicinity of Fort De Russy. On the fourth of May, the *Albatross, Estrella,* and *Arizona* were directed to make a reconnaisance up the river to ascertain whether or not the fort had been abandoned. Much to their surprise they found the fort protected by two armed steamers, the *Grand Duke* and the *Mary T,* an armed cavalry, and 30 to 40 riflemen on the opposite bank. Actually the Confederate units were in the process of removing heavy guns and supplies from the fort. These items had been placed aboard a barge and were being carried upstream by the steamer *Countess* in accordance with Taylor's instructions.[31]

A sharp engagement followed with the naval vessels

blasting away at each other from a distance of about 500 yards. After forty minutes of fighting, Lt. Commander John Hart aboard the *Albatross* ordered his fleet to withdraw reporting that the *Estrella* and *Arizona* did not assist him in battle, that he feared the safety of his own men and that his boat was damaged severely. Two of his men were reported killed and four wounded during the battle while the Confederates aboard the two vessels declared that 21 men were wounded and missing.[32]

On the afternoon of May 7th while Weitzel and Dwight were bivouacked at the beautiful home of Governor Moore, located about 12 miles below Alexandria, cavalry scouts reported that Porter and his gunboats had already cast anchor in the river near the city. The desire to be first in the city fired up Banks' troops to the point where regiments broke camp and began racing to Alexandria. Banks' units entered the municipality at about 10 o'clock that night with Weitzel leading the way.[33] So completely exhausted were the men that they dropped to the ground almost at the moment they received the order to halt—and they went to sleep wherever they fell.[34]

The Union forces lay on their backs until 10 o'clock the following morning and it wasn't until noon that they began stirring around taking a look at the city. They found Alexandria to be quite attractive with a large population of around fifteen thousand inhabitants. In the broad shallow Red River they found the gunboats *Benton, Lafayette, Estrella* and the cotton-clad ram *Switzerland.*[35]

During this period General Taylor was stricken with grief at the unwelcome news revealing the death of his two sons who were victims of scarlet fever. The two remaining children, who were girls and much older and stronger, survived. Mrs. Taylor had just reached Shreveport when the sicknesses occurred and General Taylor was saddened even more because he could not be by her side during this critical period. He wrote, "I was stunned by this intelligence, so unexpected, and it was well perhaps that the absorbing character of my duties left no time for the indulgence of private grief; but it was sad to think of the afflicted mother, alone with her dead and dying, deprived of the consolation of my presence. Many days passed before we met and then for only an hour."[36]

CHAPTER XII

VICTORY

General Banks didn't stay around Alexandria very long nor did he desire to follow Taylor's forces toward Shreveport. He explained to General-In-Chief Halleck that the Red River was falling and would soon be so low that Porter's fleet would be unable to descend—and thereby Banks' army would be operating without naval protection. The general did mention that chasing Taylor would take up too much time and that he wanted to use this time "more advantageously in another enterprise nearer at hand and more decisive in its results." No doubt he meant the reduction of Port Hudson, a goal he had set many months before.[1]

Taylor in the meantime was located at Natchitoches and was promised reinforcements in the way of men and supplies. Additional troops were to include a brigade of Texas infantry from Niblets Bluff and Major General J. C. Walker's division, 5,000 strong, which would approach the area by way of Monroe.[2]

Kirby Smith ordered Taylor to employ this force in some attempt to relieve Vicksburg which was presently be-

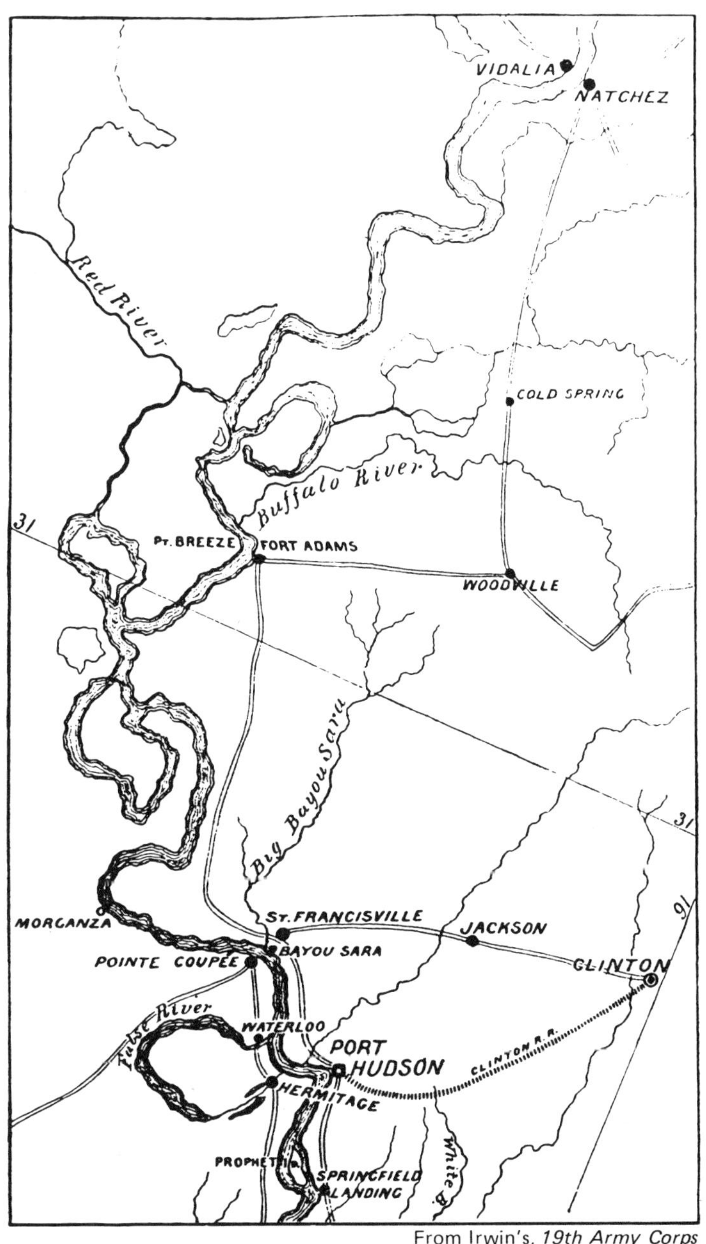

From Irwin's, *19th Army Corps*

MAP OF PORT HUDSON AREA

ing besieged by General U. S. Grant. Taylor was not too happy about this assignment because he had a fixed opinion that Vicksburg was in a peculiar situation and approaching the Mississippi by way of the west bank was almost an impossibility. He pointed out the pitfalls of "traversing the narrow peninsula opposite the place, seven miles in length and swept by guns afloat on both sides." Taylor felt that this plan was a wasted effort and stated that with Walker's force, he could recapture Berwick Bay, overrun the Lafourche, and interrupt Banks' communication with New Orleans. He stipulated, however, "that to go two hundred miles and more away from the proper theatre of action in search of an indefinite something was hard; but orders are orders."[3]

Consequently Taylor directed his forces to move opposite Vicksburg and succeeded in uprooting two fortified Union camps on the west bank of the Mississippi which were occupied by Negro troops. However, the gunboats on the river protected the fleeing troops from being captured. A frustrated Taylor, feeling that valuable time was wasted in this assignment, ordered Walker to head back to Monroe. Walker's forces would then board steamers and return to Alexandria where they would be met by Taylor. But Kirby Smith reached Monroe first and countermanded Taylor's orders sending Walker back into the region east of the Tensas River.[4]

Banks received two dispatches from General Grant. The first dated April 23rd stated that he could spare 20,000 men provided Banks could supply them. The other dispatch dated May 5th proposed sending an army corps to Bayou Sara by May 25th provided that after the reduction of Port Hudson Banks would send all the troops he could spare to Vicksburg. Although Banks consented to the offer, he was informed by a dispatch dated May 10th that Grant had crossed the Mississippi, landing his forces at Grand Gulf, and was in close pursuit of the enemy. Under these circumstances Banks felt that Grant could not retrace his steps and send the forces he had promised and too, Grant was expecting Banks to join him at Vicksburg.[5]

Banks wrote that he had three choices open to his command: "First, to pursue the enemy to Shreveport which would be without public advantage, as his army had been captured or completely routed; secondly, to join General Grant at Vicksburg; and thirdly, to invest Port Hudson with such forces as I had at my command."

After a multitude of explaining, Banks concluded that he would move immediately against Port Hudson and take his chances on the reduction of that post.[6]

(Author's note: Down through the ages, generals, hard-headed as most are, have managed to hang on to their pet projects in spite of the wishes of the higher command. There was certainly no exception in our two main characters in this arena of warfare. It was apparent from the very beginning that Banks had his mind set on taking Port Hudson and was not interested in pursuing the Vicksburg affair. Taylor was irritated to no end that he was ordered into the Vicksburg struggle but he later got around to doing exactly what he wanted to do—and that was another chance at regaining the bayou country of Louisiana.)

Part of Banks' strategy was to strip the people of the Teche country of nearly all of their precious possessions in the way of food, livestock, wagons, boats, supplies, and other materials. Of course, gathering the Negro labor and enticing the slaves to leave the plantation was perhaps the most devastating act to employ against the citizenry.

On April 20, 1863, Colonel Thomas E. Chickering of the 41st Regiment of the Massachusetts Volunteers was appointed as military governor of Opelousas and Lt. Colonel Lorenze Sargent was made provost marshal.[7]

In the weeks that followed, the Union's gathering system was stepped up and the heaping stacks of booty were stowed temporarily in the Opelousas-Port Barre area. It was stated that all this property was "saved" for the general government and was to be sent to New Orleans. Transportation facilities began to funnel into the storage areas and one such example was that the 159th New York Volunteers delivered a wagon train from Berwick all the way to Barre's Landing which was six miles east of Opelousas. Steamers were also brought into the loading stations from the far reaches of the Teche and from streams in the Atchafalaya basin.[8] On the 3rd of May, the big transport *Quinnebaug,* struggling to navigate upstream in the Teche, arrived at the wreck of the *Hart* below New Iberia and tied up to the bank, while a gang of workmen tried to clear the channel of the mass of iron and timber which the scuttled gunboat had formed. The 114th New York Regiment, who were aboard at the time, moved off the crowded deck and rested on the bank under an umbrella of magnolias.[9]

The following day the wreck was still pretty much obstructing the bayou and the regiment donned their knapsacks, shouldered their guns and decided to march through New Iberia. (Author's note: The wreck of the *Hart* was not reasonably cleared out of the bayou until October 9th when explosive charges were placed under the boilers causing the iron masses to be blown almost on shore.)[10]

Banks estimated the value of the cotton and sugar that could be confiscated in the conquered region at about $10,000,000 and the Union forces, with the help of Negro labor, began loading large quantities of these commodities aboard steamers. On May 4th, a scribe of the 52nd Massachusetts Volunteers wrote the following in his diary: "Our men have been busy at Barre's Landing bringing in cotton. More than 4,000 bales have been brought in and sent by boat to New Orleans. Our regiment has dwindled away almost to a point. We are like a big snake with the head here, the folds at New Iberia, Brashear City, Bayou Boeuf and New Orleans, and the tail at Baton Rouge."[11]

On May 7th he wrote this: "We are in fine, level country. I have not seen a hill or stone since I came into the state. The land is fertile, bears great crops of cotton, corn, and sugar cane and produces more alligators, snakes, lizards, scorpions, negroes to the acre than any other state in the Union. There have been three thousand colored people brought here since we came."[12]

Having seen the last steamer load of cotton on its way down the bayou to Brashear City, Colonel Chickering gathered the remnants on hand and loaded them into three or four hundred wagons. He left Barre's Landing on the 21st of May accompanied by his own regiment, the 41st Massachusetts; the 52nd Massachusetts Infantry; 114th, 125th and 90th New York; 22nd and 26th Maine, and a section of Nims' Massachusetts Battery.[13]

Chickering, who was Berwick-bound with this booty, was probably leading the longest and most unusual wagon train that ever passed across the bayou country of Louisiana. Irwin remarked that "this was perhaps the most curious column ever put in motion since that which defiled after Noah into the ark."[14]

The train as it moved out on the road was nearly six miles in length. This included a large column of army wagons, some of which carried ammunition, then wagons of various sorts and sizes. Negroes in large numbers, men, women and children were interspersed within the limits of the "freedom train." There were beds and bedding, household furniture and cooking utensils, cows, geese, corn, cotton, tobacco, sugar, molasses and other articles too numerous to mention. Fifty of the best army wagons in the department carried a large supply of army stores. Following this train were five hundred emigrant wagons. In addition, there were droves of horses, mules and beeves, captured from the enemy. Next there were about six thousand Negroes who had their belongings piled high on some of the wagons and who were to find employment either in Lafourche country, or at New Orleans, or as servants in the Union army.[15]

Colonel Chickering chose the eastern bank of Bayou Teche as being the safest route for the long burdensome train, and efforts were made to evade the Rebel troops which were reportedly circulating in the Vermilion area.[16]

The 114th New York met Chickering at the bayou junction at Parks and the Yankees were continuing their wanton practice of confiscating slaves, materials and foodstuffs. Nearly every hour throngs of Negroes joined the swelling column as each plantation furnished its quota to the black multitude. Although the planters devised every means to conceal their slaves, the Union invaders employed cunning methods in finding them and persuading the blacks to join the cavalcade.[17]

One such example was recorded by Harris Beecher. A Union soldier discovered that some Negroes were making signals of distress from an attic window and upon examination discovered that a large number of slaves had been locked in the garret to prevent them from running off with the Yankees. A ladder was quickly improvised and placed upon the window whereby men, women and children climbed down "to seek protection under the flag of freedom."

According to Beecher the planters were thunderstruck at the infidelity of their servants and vehemently objected to the "audacity of the blackhearted abolitionists."[18]

The author felt that Beecher's interesting description of Chickering's train on May 23rd below St. Martinville was worth mentioning:

> "In the history of the war, it is probable that another such sight was never witnessed. There can be no doubt that this was the greatest multitude of contrabands ever collected. Every few minutes the boys would burst into shouts of merriment as some new scene especially ludicrous or ridiculous presented itself. Here came a mammoth plantation cart filled with rough furniture, and screaming children, nearly nude, drawn by a pair of oxen. Then came a young man leading a cow, upon whose horns and back was attached a rattling museum of frying pans, pails, gridirons, old clothes and hoes. Next appeared a creaking wagon, in which was an old grey-haired couple, demurely sitting on a broken stove. Then came trudging along a bevy of barefooted women with infants, papoose-like on their backs. Presently a very ancient and ragged looking mule with two or three women and children astride its back.[19]
>
> "Again would appear more plantation carts covered with awnings of blankets, cowhides or boards. Then the attention would be attracted to an old man limping along on a cane and carrying a half naked child astride his neck. Or the eye would fall upon a young wench,

walking stiff and erect, with an enormous bundle poised upon her head. Occasionally an old vehicle would break down in the road and scatter in the mud the most wonderful collection of furniture, utensils, clothing, and traps generally, that the mind can conceive of. Now and then some quaint establishment would have a runaway, tearing through the black ranks, upsetting everything in its mad career."

The slaves "were mostly clothed in coarse gray cotton suits. A few, though, were decked off with the most expensive finery, which they had stolen from their masters or mistresses. All the women wore gaudy colored bandanas, wrapped over their woolly pates, and the men generally had broad brimmed straw hats, much the worse for wear."[20]

A humorous incident was disclosed by J. P. Moore of the 52nd Massachusetts as the Federal cavalcade passed through St. Martinville. "Two ladies were sitting very haughtily" on their upper gallery observing the passersby. Suddenly their colored "mammy" weighing about 250 pounds rushed out of the lower part of the house and set out to join the parade. "Suddenly the haughtiness of the fine ladies on the gallery changed. They flashed down the inner stairs, rushed to the very edge of the street, got each a fat arm of their household reliance and sought to drag her back to the house. The soldiers cheered both sides but the ladies prevailed."[21]

In the meantime Taylor with hardly a thousand troops was still encamped at Natchitoches with scouts in the vicinity of Alexandria observing the operations of the enemy. Mouton and Green, having obtained supplies at the Sabine, returned to the Teche country too late to cut off Chickering's train.[22]

At four o'clock in the afternoon of May 23rd, Chickering and company crossed the Bayou Teche at New Iberia and bivouacked about one mile below in the vicinity of Nelson's Canal. On the following day the colonel led his train and forces through Jeanerette, Franklin and then decided to encamp for the night at Centerville.[23] Suddenly a frightened mass of stragglers and Negroes came running down the road shouting "The Rebels are coming!" which almost caused a panic. It was reported that the rear guard was attacked near Franklin by a large Rebel cavalry force believed to be that of General Green.[24] (Note: Colonel Green was promoted to brigadier general on May 20, 1863)

Chickering, feeling insecure because his sparsely protected wagon train could be smashed during the night, had his troops fall in at 10:00 p.m. and move on towards Berwick with great rapidity. It is believed that this move foiled a planned Rebel attack and the Union troops, weary from the long marches, fell in their tracks at Berwick where they were protected by gunboats and land fortifications.[25] By May 28th everything in the train had been transferred across the bay to Brashear City and then the disposal of the tremendous booty got underway.

Day by day the shores of Berwick Bay became gradually relieved of the mass confusion of entangled lives, animals and provisions. Contrabands and cotton-bales were hurried off on railway flats, while shrewd cattle-brokers, after swarming around the quartermaster's door, drove off their bargains of beeves. Mules were trotted off to army markets and plantations. Carts, chaises, family coaches, saddles, harnesses, debris of Attakapas confiscation, were invoiced, via rail, to New Orleans auction blocks.[26]

General Banks had found Port Hudson a harder place to take than he had first realized and now it became apparent that he was ordering nearly every available regiment in the department to assist him in his operation. Consequently, the Federal troops in the Teche country began thinning out, leaving the door wide open for Taylor to replan his strategy for a bayou country acquisition.[27]

Brashear City, however, was protected by the wide expanse of water at Berwick Bay, the gunboat *Hollyhock,* strong fortifications, a large quantity of supplies and ammunition and an armed force which was made up of several regiments. There were: one unit of the 21st Indiana; four companies of the 23rd Connecticut; two companies of the

176th New York, and one company of the 42nd Massachusetts Infantry.

At Alexandria, Taylor devised a plan whereby he proposed to attack the Lafourche and Teche country by two different fronts with such effctiveness that Banks would be forced to abandon his siege upon Port Hudson.[28] The Confederate general planned to move a force through Plaquemine and Thibodaux and then attack Brashear City from the rear, while along the Teche and Atchafalaya another detachment would move against Brashear City's front.[29] A target date was to be set for the simultaneous attack upon Brashear City from both fronts.

Besides Brashear City, the Union command had detachments posted at Plaquemine, Donaldsonville, New Orleans, Thibodaux and along the Western Railroad. All the rest of Banks' troops were at Port Hudson.[30]

Taylor welcomed the arrival of three small Texas cavalry regiments numbering around 650 men and ordered Colonel J. P. Major, the senior officer, to move his force to Morgan's Ferry on the Atchafalaya. This began the upper thrust of Taylor's plan. The general then boarded an ambulance, and, by using a relay of mules, arrived in the lower Teche country within a matter of a few hours. He met with Generals Mouton and Green and laid out the procedure for the drive in that area.[31]

Taylor directed the two generals to collect small boats of every description that they could find and to impress upon everyone that the secrecy of the upcoming mission was of the utmost importance. The plan was no doubt one of the most daring on record. Volunteer Rebels would man the "Mosquito Fleet," as it was later called, and navigate the lakes and bayous above Brashear City during the night, landing secretly in the rear of the town. At dawn cannonading from the Berwick side would draw the attention of the Yanks to the Berwick front and then the "Mosquito Fleet" men would set off a surprise attack upon the garrison. Taylor then returned to meet Colonel Major and engaged in a movement which carried them down the Fordoche and Grosse Tete Bayous to "Fausse Reviere."[32]

Green's brigade, which was encamped about four miles above the old Bisland battlefield, immediately began collecting and making small boats. No one was told what the activity was all about and naturally everyone was curious.[33]

It took several days for Green's men to assemble the midget fleet which consisted of 53 vessels which included skiffs, bateaux, dugouts, flats, "sugar-coolers," etc. The largest floating unit was a big skiff, with double oars, that could carry fifteen passengers. It was named the *Tom Green.*[34]

Although General Green asked for two hundred and fifty volunteers over three hundred enthusiastic Confederates stepped forward. They were drawn from Green's brigade and the 2nd Louisiana Cavalry with Major Sherard Hunter of Baylor's Texans in command, assisted by Major J. D. Blair of the 2nd Louisiana.[35]

The unique armada began its strange mission at sunset on June 22nd, and the units traveled in pairs down the Bayou Teche, up the Atchafalaya, into and across Grand Lake, then eastward through timber passes, and across Flat Lake and Lake Palourde.[36]

In the meantime General Green moved his force (500 men) consisting of the 5th Texas, 2nd Louisiana Cavalry, Waller's Battalion, and the Valverde and a section of Nichols' Batteries to Cochran's sugarhouse which was located about two miles from the bay. There they left their horses and moved by foot reaching Berwick before daylight and set up their guns across from the enemy encampment.[37]

Before the "Mosquito Fleet" reached the shoreline behind Tiger Island, the entire flotilla was halted and the oarsmen directed to muffle their oars with moss so that the sneak attack would be conducted as quietly as possible. The men —except for more than 50 who lost their way because of darkness and an inability to navigate in swampy waters—landed just before daybreak.[38]

At dawn Green opened up with the Valverde battery, the first shot exploding in the middle of the enemy's encampment. Green's men fired 40 to 50 shells before the Yankees replied at all. The gunboat *Hollyhock,* which was anchored in the bay, a short distance below Green's position, opened fire. After daylight, however, the gunboat retreated downstream but kept pounding away at the Berwick shoreline with her heavy guns. The Union troops were also firing away across the bay.[39]

While Hunter's invading force was wading waist-deep through swampy terrain, they could hear the exchange of gunfire between Green's artillery and the Union defenders. However, just before they approached the enemy fortification, hesitation developed in the ranks. The men were afraid they would fall into a trap and be wiped out by Federal rifle fire and bayonets.[40]

Major Hunter grouped them and warned them that "we may all be shot." He continued, "Not one of us may get back to the brigade, but gentlemen, we'd better just fall down in our tracks than go back disgraced and have old Tom Green tell us so."

These words seemed to rally the Southerners. About 5:30 a.m. the recharged group reached open ground and were in full view of Brashear City which was approximately 800 yards away. Hunter was not quite ready to make the attack and he rested his command a few minutes and approached within 400 yards of the town by moving under cover of a skirt of timber.

At this point, they were discovered by the enemy so Hunter immediately gave the command to charge and the small armed force gave it their all, firing away like mad, and yelling at the top of their lungs. There was near confusion in the Yankee camps as the surprised men fought desperately to defend themselves. Brashear City was overwhelmed by the Rebel sneak attack and surrendered at 7:30 a.m.[41]

Hunter reported his loss as three killed and 18 wounded while the enemy suffered 46 killed, 40 wounded and 1,300 men taken prisoners. (Many of these prisoners were convalescents left behind by nearly thirty companies).[42] Hunter also captured eleven 24-pounder and 32-pounder siege guns; a 2,500 stand of small-arms (Enfield and Burnside rifles), and immense quantities of quartermaster's, commissary and ordinance stores. It was also reported that the

Rebels captured 2,000 Negroes, between 200 and 300 wagons and tents, 2 locomotives and 80 railroad cars.[43]

By this time Taylor had returned and crossed the bay in a pirogue with Green. He reported that "It was a scene of the wildest excitement and confusion. The sight of such quantities of 'loot' quite upset my hungry followers." However, order was restored when Mouton crossed with a detachment of infantry.[44]

After Green succeeded in having a sizable force of his men to cross Berwick Bay, he ordered them to mount and follow the rail toward Bayou Boeuf where Lt. Colonel A. J. Duganne of the 176th New York had retreated.[45]

Colonel Major had been quite successful in his thrust around the Atchafalaya Basin. At Plaquemine he captured 87 prisoners, burned three steamers, two steam flats, 100 bales of cotton, and garnered a large quantity of commissary stores. At Bayou Goula, Major took commissary and quartermaster's stores, destroyed Federal plantations and recaptured 1,000 negroes. 140 prisoners were taken at Paincourtville and a small force at Terre Bonne station. After experiencing still opposition and rain, he hurried on towards Brashear City for his scheduled meeting with Mouton and Green.[46]

Major arrived at Bayou Boeuf at 4:20 p.m. on June 23rd, 1863 and took possession of the east bank while the enemy (Duganne) was entrenched on the opposite bank. The 23rd was the day set by Taylor for his two Confederate forces to meet and the timing was almost perfect. Duganne was hemmed in between Major and Green and at daylight Duganne's units numbering 435 officers and men surrendered to General Green's scouts who were riding five miles ahead of their column.[47]

However, before Duganne surrendered, he made sure that he wouldn't leave another whopping prize for Taylor's invaders. He therefore "put the torch" to the big sugarhouse, located in the Bayou Boeuf area, which contained over a million dollars worth of army supplies, officers' personal effects, "loot," etc. These valuable items were stored in early April just before the Yankees began their invasion of Bisland and Irish Bend. (Author's note: The storage operation at the sugarhouse was described in more detail in Chapter 7 of this book.)[48]

But the Confederates finally garnered over two million dollars worth of booty in the campaign including those acquisitions brought in by Colonel Major.[49] General Banks on occasion had referred to Berwick Bay as "the key" during his earlier attempted conquest of Louisiana and Texas, and now, this strategic area had reverted to the original defenders.[50]

The success of this project represented a tremendous victory for one Richard Taylor who fought his heart out for the Confederacy. It actually marked the first time that the Confederate general could enjoy an abundance of supplies since his arrival in the Trans-Mississippi Department. His brave officers and men, who were constantly battling against overwhelming odds, rejoiced in their daring accomplishment and their morale was higher now than it had been for quite some time.

EPILOGUE

Taylor's triumphant return to the bayou country did boost the morale of its people and brought temporary relief to those citizens who suffered so much at the hands of ruthless Yankees. The foregoing contents of this book may be referred to as the first phase of the bayou country campaign representing a period of colorful action and interesting circumstances.

Of course, we all know that the Confederates didn't win the war but the author, being a southerner, chose to stop at this point in order to give his book a sort of happy ending. You may call it author's prerogative if you wish, but we assure you that we have tried to maintain an objective point of view throughout the twelve chapters of this manuscript.

We'd also like to point out that nearly all of the information dealing with foraging, sacking, pillaging, ravishing, and wanton destruction was taken from Yankee regimental histories and U. S. Official records. We urge the readers to digest the accounts of other historians, many of which are referenced in the back pages of this book. This will certainly broaden your knowledge of all phases of the War Between the States from both a Union and Confederate standpoint.

In our research we found that this conflict was no different than other wars. There were good and bad on both sides and brave men fought and died for a cause which they thought was right. In this Bicentennial year, when the history of our precious nation is being reviewed by its millions of citizens, we sincerely hope that careful observation is made of the tragic results of this terrible war—and that we firmly resolve and pray to God that a calamity such as this, where Americans were fighting Americans, will never, ever happen again in these United States of America.

REFERENCES

In the following notes the initials "OR" designate that the information was taken from *The Official Records of the Union and Confederate Armies,* Series 1. The initials "ORN" indicate *The Official Records of the Union and Confederate Navies,* Series 1.

FOREWORD

1. Richard Taylor, *Destruction and Reconstruction,* 105.
2. James K. Hosmer, *The Color Guard,* 116 & 117.
3. Henry Hill Goodell, *25th Connecticut Volunteers,* 63 & 64.
4. John De Forest, *A Volunteer's Adventures,* 37 & 38.

CHAPTER I
FROM THE BEGINNING

1. Edwin Davis, *Louisiana a Narrative Study.*
2. From the Weeks Papers.
3. Caffery Papers; History of Morgan City 1960 Centennial Edition.
4. Morgan City Historical Society; *A History of Morgan City.*

5. *Opelousas Daily World,* 250th Anniversary Edition, 72.
6. William Arceneaux, *Acadian General Alfred Mouton,* 39, 40 & 41.
7. *Morgan City Review,* 1960 Centennial Edition.
8. Ethel Taylor, "Discontent in Confederate Louisiana" *(Louisiana Historical Journal),* Vol. II, No. 4, p. 411.
9. *ibid.*
10. Charles Roland, *Louisiana Sugar Plantations,* 24 & 25.
11. William Arceneaux, *Acadian General,* 39.
12. Edwin Davis, *Louisiana a Narrative Study.*
13. Irwin, *History of the 19th Army Corps,* 8, 9 & 10.
14. John Winters, *The Civil War in Louisiana,* 65.
15. ORN, Vol. 18, 134.
16. ORN. Vol. 18, 152, 164, 185 & 330.
17. Charles F. Roland, *Louisiana Sugar Plantations During the Civil War,* 49.
18. *ibid.*
19. *Opelousas Daily World,* 250th Anniversary Edition, 58.
20. Ethel Taylor, *Discontent in Confederate Louisiana,* Vol. II, No. 4, 412.
21. Davis, *Louisiana a Narrative History,* 256.
22. Barnes F. Lathrop, *The Pugh Plantation 1860-1865* (A study of Life in Lower Louisiana), 161.
23. *ibid,* 166.
24. *ibid,* 167.
25. OR, Vol. XV, 563.
26. *ibid,* 426.
27. *ibid,* 906 & 907.
28. *ibid.*
29. *ibid,* 568 & 569.

CHAPTER II
GENERAL TAYLOR ARRIVES

1. OR, Vol. XV, 789.
2. Richard Taylor, *Destruction and Reconstruction,* 99 & 102.

3. OR, Vol. XV, 919.
4. *ibid;* OR, Vol. VI, Series 2, 814.
5. Richard Taylor, *Destruction and Reconstruction,* 117.
6. *ibid,* 118.
7. *ibid,* 111; Winters, *The Civil War in Louisiana,* 155 & 156.
8. Charles Spurlin, *West of the Mississippi with Waller's 13th Texas Cavalry Battalion,* 2 & 3; Winters, *The Civil War in Louisiana,* 155; Taylor, *Destruction and Reconstruction,* 111.
9. OR, Vol. XV, 133.
10. Geo. Carpenter, *History of the 8th Vermont,* 63, 64 & 65.
11. Taylor, *Destruction and Reconstruction,* 112.
12. OR, Vol. XV, 133.
13. Spurlin, *West of the Mississippi with Waller,* 48.
14. OR, Vol. XV, 133.
15. Irwin, *History of the 19th Army Corps,* 46.
16. OR, Vol. XV, 133.
17. Irwin, *The History of the 19th Army Corps,* 45 & 46; De Forest, *A Volunteer's Adventures,* 53.
18. *ibid;* OR, Vol. XV, 176.
19. Irwin, *The History of the 19th Army Corps,* 46.
20. OR, Vol. XV, 159.
21. *ibid.*
22. *ibid.*
23. *ibid.*
24. Irwin, *History of the 19th Army Corps,* 46.
25. William Arceneaux, *Acadian General Alfred Mouton,* 53 & 54.
26. Taylor, *Destruction and Reconstruction,* 113.
27. Spurlin, *West of the Mississippi with Waller,* 55.
28. OR, Vol. XV, 176.
29. William Arceneaux, *Acadian General Alfred Mouton,* 54.

CHAPTER III

THE INVASION OF LAFOURCHE

1. ORN, Vol. 19, 316 & 317; OR, Vol. XV, 166 & 167; DeForest, *A Volunteer's Adventures,* 55.
2. OR, Vol. XV, 167.
3. OR, Vol. XV, 176.
4. OR, Vol. XV, 176 & 177.
5. DeForest, *A Volunteer's Adventures.*
6. OR, Vol. XV, 177.
7. *ibid.*
8. *ibid.,* 178.
9. ORN, Vol. 19, 330; De Forest, *A Volunteer's Adventures,* 73.
10. Charles Johnson, *Muskets and Medicine,* 44.
11. ORN, Vol. 19, 326.
12. De Forest, *A Volunteer's Adventures,* 73.
13. OR, Vol. XV, 179.
14. ORN, Vol. 19, 326.
15. OR, Vol. XV, 179.
16. *ibid.*
17. ORN, Vol. 19, 327.
18. Taylor, *Destruction and Reconstruction,* 119.
19. B. F. Queen's report in *Franklin Banner Tribune,* Historical issue, April 28, 1959; ORN, Series II, Vol. 1, 251.
20. ORN, Vol. 19, 335.
21. *ibid;* OR, Vol. XV, 186.
22. ORN, Vol. 19, 335.
23. Harris Beecher, *Record of the 114th Regiment New York Volunteers,* 118.
24. De Forest, *A Volunteer's Adventures,* 78.
25. Frank Flinn, *Campaigning with Banks,* 30.
26. Gouverneur Morris, *History of a Volunteer Regiment,* 92 & 93.
27. ORN, Vol. 19, 327.
28. ORN, Vol. 19, 332.
29. George Carpenter, *History of the 8th Regiment Vermont Vols,* 71.

30. ORN, Vol. 19, 332.
31. OR, Vol. XV, 170.
32. *ibid,* 171 & 172.
33. *ibid,* 162.
34. *ibid,* 172.
35. *ibid,* 856-860.
36. *ibid,* 860.
37. Evans, *Confederate Military History,* Vol. 10, 315.

CHAPTER IV

GUNBOATS ON THE TECHE

1. Charles Dufour's paper, "The Salt Mine at Avery Island."
2. *History of Avery Island Salt Mine.*
3. *ibid.*
4. Taylor, *Destruction and Reconstruction,* 114.
5. Ella Lonn, *Salt As a Factor in the Confederacy,* 93; OR, Vol. XV, 175 & 186.
6. OR, Vol. XV, 184.
7. ORN, Vol. 19, 328.
8. OR, Vol. XV, 179.
9. Irwin, *History of the 19th Army Corps,* 94.
10. ORN, Vol. 19, 327 & 328; OR, Vol. XV, 186 & 187.
11. ORN, Vol. 19, 327; OR, Vol. XV, 186.
12. ORN, Vol. 19, 328.
13. OR, Vol. XV, 187.
14. ORN, Vol. 19, 337.
15. OR, Vol. XV, 187.
16. ORN, Vol. 19, 328.
17. OR, Vol. XV, 187; ORN, Vol. 19, 329 & 331.
18. ORN, Vol.19, 334 & 337.
19. ORN, Vol. 19, 328 & 329.
20. ORN, Vol. 19, 331.
21. From the Jackson, Mississippi, *The Daily Southern Crisis,* Jan. 24, 1863.
22. Harris Beecher, *History of the 114th Regiment,* N.Y. Vols., 120.
23. OR, Vol. XV, 1088.

24. *ibid.*
25. *ibid.*
26. *ibid.*
27. The Jackson, Mississippi, *The Daily Southern Crisis,* Jan. 24, 1863.
28. *ibid.*

CHAPTER V
THE *COTTON* FALLS

1. Irwin, *History of the 19th Army Corps,* 52, 55, 56 & 60.
2. Clement Evans, *Military History of Louisiana,* Vol. 10, 88.
3. Irwin, *History of the 19th Army Corps,* 62, 63 & 64.
4. ORN, Vol. 19, 494 & 495.
5. *ibid,* 506 & 551.
6. Taylor, *Destruction & Reconstruction,* 119 & 120; OR, Vol. XV, 873.
7. Clement Evans, *Military History of Louisiana,* Vol. 10, 82.
8. *ibid,* 83; OR, Vol. XV, 234 & 235.
9. Geo. Carpenter, *History of the 8th Vermont Volunteers,* 83 & 84.
10. ORN, Vol. 19, 518.
11. OR, Vol. XV, 1089.
12. ORN, Vol. 19, 517, 518, 519 & 520.
13. ORN, Vol. 19, 521-524.
14. *ibid;* Taylor, *Destruction & Reconstruction,* 121.
15. Geo. Carpenter, *History of the 8th Vermont Volun-*teers, 87 & 88.
16. *ibid.*
17. Taylor, *Destruction & Reconstruction,* 121.
18. Geo. Carpenter, *History of the 8th Vermont Volun-*teers, 89.
19. ORN, Vol. 19, 525.
20. OR, Vol. XV, 234.
21. *ibid,* 240.
22. *ibid.*

23. OR, Vol. XV, 676 & 677.
24. *ibid,* 243 & 244.
25. *ibid.*
26. OR, Vol. XV, 246, 248, 249 & 250.
27. Irwin, *History of the 19th Army Corps,* 87.

CHAPTER VI

CAPTURE OF THE *DIANA*

1. Harris Beecher, *History of the 114th Regiment New York Volunteers,* 120; ORN, Vol. 19, 624 & 625.
2. ORN, Vol. 19, 624 & 625.
3. *ibid,* 624, 625, 626.
4. OR, Vol. XV, 972.
5. John Winters, *The Civil War in Louisiana,* 221.
6. OR, Vol. XV, 1005.
7. ORN, Vol. 19, 640.
8. A. J. Duganne, *Twenty Months in the Department of the Gulf,* 195.
9. *ibid,* 195 & 196.
10. John Fisk Allen, *Memorial of Pickering Dodge Allen,* 98.
11. *ibid,* 93 & 98.
12. *ibid;* Duganne, *Twenty Months in the Department of the Gulf,* 189.
13. Duganne, *Twenty Months in the Department of the Gulf,* 197.
14. *ibid,* 199; John Allen, *Memorial of Pickering Dodge Allen,* 98 & 99.
15. Duganne's *Twenty Months in the Department of the Gulf,* 200; Allen's *Memorial of Pickering Allen,* 99 & 100.
16. A. J. Duganne, *Twenty Months in the Deparment of the Gulf,* 200 & 201.
17. Allen, *Memorial of Pickering Allen,* 101 & 102.
18. A. J. Duganne, *Twenty Months in the Department of the Gulf,* 201.
19. ORN, Vol. 20, 112.

20. Duganne, *Twenty Months in the Department of the Gulf,* 201; Allen, *Memorial of Pickering Allen,* 102.
21. ORN, Vol. 20, 109 & 113.
22. *ibid,* 113.
23. ORN, Vol. 20, 109 & 110.
24. *ibid,* 112 & 113; Frank Flinn, *Campaigning with Banks,* 32.
25. ORN, Vol. 20, 113.
26. ORN. Vol. 19, 699.
27. OR, Vol. XV, 258.

CHAPTER VII

THE BATTLE OF BISLAND

1. OR, Vol. XV, 386; Irwin, *19th Army Corps,* 89; James Hall,*Cayuga in the Field,* 90.
2. Irwin, *19th Army Corps,* 89.
3. William Tiemann, *159th Regiment New York Volunteers,* 27; A. J. Duganne, *Twenty Months in the Department of the Gulf,* 157.
4. OR, Vol. XV, 294; Harris Beecher, *History of the 114th New York Volunteers,* 134.
5. Beecher, *History of the 114th New York Volunteers,* 134 & 135.
6. Irwin, *19th Army Corps,* 90 & 91.
7. OR, Vol. XV, 294.
8. Irwin, *19th Army Corps,* 91; Beecher, *History of the 114th New York Volunteers,* 137.
9. OR, Vol. XV, 388.
10. Flinn, *Campaigning with Banks,* 33 & 34.
11. Beecher, *History of the 114th New York Volunteers,* 138 & 139.
12. *ibid;* Irwin, *19th Army Corps,* 91.
13. Flinn, *Campaigning with Banks,* 35.
14. OR, Vol. XV, 386; James Hall, *Cayuga in the Field,* 90.
15. OR, Vol. XV, 396 & 397.
16. Beecher, *History of the 114th New York Volunteers,* 139.

17. *ibid.*
18. Flinn, *Campaigning with Banks,* 37.
19. Beecher, *History of the 114th New York Volunteers,* 140; De Forest, *A Volunteer's Adventure,* 87.
20. Flinn, *Campaigning with Banks,* 42.
21. James Hall, *Cayuga in the Field,* 91 & 92.
22. Winters, *The Civil War in Louisiana,* 224.
23. OR, Vol. XV, 388 & 389.
24. *ibid.*
25. Beecher, *History of the 114th New York Volunteers,* 141.
26. Taylor, *Destruction & Reconstruction,* 130.
27. James Hall, *Cayuga in the Field,* 92.
28. Taylor, *Destruction & Reconstruction,* 130.
29. Hall, *Cayuga in the Field,* 92 & 93.
30. OR, Vol. XV, 390.
31. *ibid;* OR, Vol. 53, 463; Taylor, *Destruction & Reconstruction,* 131; Newman, *The Maryland Semmes,* 92.
32. Taylor, *Destruction & Reconstruction,* 130.
33. *ibid,* 131.
34. *ibid;* OR, Vol. XV, 390.
35. Flinn, *Campaigning with Banks,* 53 & 54; OR, Vol. XV, 347.
36. Irwin, *19th Army Corps,* 100.
37. *ibid,* 101.
38. Taylor, *Destruction & Reconstruction,* 132.
39. *ibid,* 132 & 133.
40. *ibid.*

CHAPTER VIII
THE BATTLE OF IRISH BEND

1. James Hosmer, *The Color Guard,* 125.
2. *ibid,* 126.
3. Henry Goodell, *25th Connecticut Volunteers,* 33 & 34.
4. James Ewer, *3rd Massachusetts Cavalry,* 70; OR, Vol. XV, 358.
5. Ewer, *3rd Massachusetts Cavalry,* 70.
6. OR, Vol. XV, 377; Irwin, *19th Army Corps,* 105.

7. OR, Vol. XV, 271; Irwin, *19th Army Corps,* 105.
8. Irwin, *19th Army Corps,* 106.
9. *ibid;* OR, Vol. XV, 358, 359, 364 & 371.
10. OR, Vol. XV, 364; OR, Vol. 53, 466.
11. OR, Vol. XV, 359.
12. OR, Vol. XV, 364.
13. *ibid,* 359.
14. OR, Vol. 53, 466.
15. *ibid.*
16. *ibid.*
17. OR, Vol. XV, 371.
18. Irwin, *19th Army Corps,* 107.
19. OR, Vol. XV, 359.
20. Homer Sprague, *History of the 13th Connecticut,* 110.
21. Irwin, "19th Army Corps" (map).
22. Mrs. Thomas Holmes, *Oaklawn Manor.*
23. J. F. Moors, *History of the 52nd Massachusetts,* 116; Hosmer, *The Color Guard,* 130 & 131.
24. William Tiemann, *159th Regiment New York Volunteers,* 29.
25. OR, Vol. XV, 383 & 384.
26. *ibid;* Irwin, *19th Army Corps,* 110.
27. Henry Goodell, *25th Connecticut Volunteers,* 35.
28. Irwin, *19th Army Corps,* 110.
29. *ibid,* 111.
30. *ibid;* OR, Vol. XV, 384; Goodell, *25th Connecticut Volunteers,* 37.
31. Goodell, *25th Connecticut Volunteers,* 37.
32. Taylor, *Destruction & Reconstruction,* 133; OR, Vol. XV, 392.
33. Sprague, *History of the 13th Connecticut,* 113.
34. *ibid,* 113 & 114.
35. Hosmer, *The Color Guard,* 133 & 134.
36. Goodell, *25th Connecticut Volunteers,* 38.
37. Tiemann, *159th Regiment New York Volunteers,* 30 & 31.
38. OR, Vol. XV, 372.

39. Sprague, *History of the 13th Connecticut,* 114, 115 & 116.
40. *ibid,* 116, 117 & 118.
41. OR, Vol. XV, 392.
42. *ibid.*
43. OR, Vol. 53, 464, 465.
44. OR, Vol. XV, 392.
45. *ibid,* 399; Irwin, *19th Army Corps,* 115.
46. Beecher, *History of the 114th New York Volunteers,* 152.
47. Ewer, *3rd Massachusetts Cavalry,* 74.
48. Irwin, *19th Army Corps,* 115 & 116.
49. *ibid.*
50. Cecil Eby, Jr., *A Virginia Yankee in the Civil War,* 168, (University of North Carolina Press).
51. OR, Vol. XV, 393 & 399.
52. Irwin, *19th Army Corps,* 102.
53. *ibid,* 116.
54. *ibid,* 121 & 122; ORN, Vol. 20, 137 & 138.
55. ORN, Vol. 20, 137 & 138.
56. *ibid;* Irwin, *19th Army Corps,* 121 & 122; B. F. Queen's letter to John Caffery in *Franklin Banner Tribune* Historical Edition, April 28, 1959.

CHAPTER IX
THE AFTERMATH

1. *Franklin Banner Tribune,* Historical Edition, April 28, 1959; John Caffery's account, Section 3, p. 2.
2. Sprague, *History of the 13th Connecticut Volunteers,* 122.
3. *Franklin Banner Tribune,* Historical issue.
4. Sprague, *History of the 13th Connecticut Volunteers,* 122.
5. J. F. Moors, *History of the 52nd Massachusetts Regiment,* 117.
6. *ibid,* 120.
7. Tiemann, *159th Regiment New York Volunteers,* 30; Flinn, *Campaigning with Banks,* 59 & 60.

8. OR, Vol. XV, 392 & 393.
9. *ibid.*
10. OR, Vol. XV, 1093-1095.
11. OR, Vol. XV, 1049.
12. *ibid,* 398-399.
13. Beecher, *History of the 114th New York Volunteers,* 148.
14. *ibid,* 149.
15. *ibid,* 150.
16. Irwin, *19th Army Corps,* 122.
17. Beecher, *History of the 114th New York Volunteers,* 154.
18. *ibid,* 154 & 155.
19. *ibid,* 154.
20. Cecil Eby, *A Virginia Yankee in the Civil War,* 169. (University of North Carolina Press).
21. *ibid,* 171.
22. *ibid.*
23. Harry Wright Newman, *The Maryland Semmes and Kindred Families,* 92 & 93.

CHAPTER X
DESTRUCTION OF THE SALT WORKS

1. OR, Vol. XV, 393.
2. Irwin, *19th Army Corps,* 123; John Allen, *Memorial of Pickering Dodge Allen,* 112.
3. John Allen, *Memorial of Pickering Dodge Allen,* 112 & 113; OR, Vol. XV, 393.
4. OR, Vol. XV, 343.
5. *ibid,* 343 & 344.
6. *ibid.*
7. The Weeks Papers, Iberia Parish Library, page 13.
8. *ibid.*
9. OR, Vol. XV, 373 & 393.
10. Carleton's, *Stories of Our Soldiers,* 181.
11. OR, Vol. XV, 382.
12. *ibid.*

13. Caroline Whitcomb, *History of the 2nd Massachusetts Battery,* 45.
14. From *The Era,* New Orleans, Louisiana, June 16, 1863.
15. *ibid.*
16. *ibid.*
17. Weeks Papers, New Iberia Library, 9.
18. *ibid,* 9 & 10.
19. J. F. Moors, *History of the 52nd Massachusetts Regiment,* 153.
20. *ibid,* 154.
21. *ibid.*
22. Frank Moore, *Rebellion Record,* Vol. VI, 542.
23. Charles Johnson, *Muskets and Medicine,* 150.
24. From Dulcito brochure.
25. From *Sunday Iberian,* May 2, 1971, 26.
26. Weeks Papers, New Iberia Library, 10 & 11; Moors, *History of the 52nd Massachusetts,* 158.
27. *ibid.*

CHAPTER XI

THE BATTLE OF VERMILION BRIDGE

1. James Hall, *Cayuga in the Field,* 98.
2. OR, Vol. XV, 373.
3. *ibid;* Gouverneur Morris, *History of a Volunteer Regiment,* 103.
4. Goodell, *25th Connecticut Volunteers,* 61.
5. *ibid.*
6. Irwin, *19th Army Corps,* 128.
7. *ibid,* 128 & 129.
8. Morris, *History of a Volunteer Regiment,* 107 & 108.
9. Beecher, *History of the 114th New York Volunteers,* 170.
10. *ibid.*
11. Hall, *Cayuga in the Field,* 99.
12. Beecher, *History of the 114th New York Volunteers,* 170 & 171.
13. *ibid.*

14. Hall, *Cayuga in the Field,* 99; Winters, *Civil War in Louisiana,* 233.
15. ORN, Vol. 20, 153.
16. *ibid,* 153 & 154.
17. *ibid,* 154.
18. *ibid.*
19. Irwin, *19th Army Corps,* 126.
20. OR, Vol. XV, 1095 & 1096.
21. Hall, *Cayuga in the Field,* 100.
22. Hosmer, *The Color Guard,* 149 & 150.
23. Beecher, *History of the 114th New York Volunteers,* 172.
24. *ibid.*
25. Irwin, *19th Army Corps,* 144.
26. *ibid,* 145.
27. *ibid,* 146.
28. OR, Vol. XV, 948.
29. *ibid,* 1054.
30. Taylor, *Destruction & Reconstruction,* 136.
31. ORN, Vol. 20, 78, 79 & 91.
32. *ibid,* 81, 82 & 83.
33. Irwin, *19th Army Corps,* 147.
34. Hall, *Cayuga in the Field,* 103.
35. *ibid,* 103 & 104.
36. Taylor, *Destruction and Reconstruction,* 136 & 137.

CHAPTER XII
VICTORY

1. OR, Vol. XV, 313.
2. *ibid,* 1081 & 1082.
3. Taylor, *Destruction & Reconstruction,* 138.
4. *ibid,* 139.
5. OR, Vol. XXVI, 11 & 12.
6. *ibid,* 12.
7. Ewer, *3rd Massachusetts Cavalry,* 77.
8. *ibid,* 78; Tiemann, *History of the 159th New York Volunteers,* 37.

9. Beecher, *History of the 114th New York Volunteers,* 167 & 168.
10. OR, Vol. XXVI, 380.
11. Moors, *52nd Regiment Massachusetts Volunteers,* 134, 135, 136 & 137.
12. *ibid,* 137.
13. Ewer, *3rd Massachusetts Cavalry,* 82 & 83.
14. Irwin, *19th Army Corps,* 156 & 157.
15. Ewer, *3rd Massachusetts Cavalry,* 81 & 82.
16. *ibid,* 83; Beecher, *History of the 114th New York,* 183.
17. Beecher, *History of the 114th New York,* 182 & 183.
18. *ibid.*
19. *ibid,* 185.
20. *ibid,* 186.
21. Moors, *History of the 152nd Massachusetts,* 143 & 144.
22. Taylor, *Destruction & Reconstruction,* 137.
23. Ewer, *3rd Massachusetts Cavalry,* 85.
24. Beecher, *History of the 114th New York,* 187 & 188.
25. *ibid,* 189; Ewer, *3rd Massachusetts Cavalry,* 84 & 85; OR, XXVI, Part 1, 41; Flinn, *Campaigning with Banks,* 71.
26. Duganne, *Twenty Months in the Department of the Gulf,* 102.
27. Ewer, *3rd Massachusetts Cavalry,* 86.
28. OR, Vol. XXVI, Part 1, 209 & 210.
29. Flinn, *Campaigning with Banks,* 88 & 89.
30. *ibid.*
31. Taylor, *Destruction & Reconstruction,* 139 & 140.
32. *ibid;* Theo Noel, *A Campaign from Santa Fe to the Mississippi,* 82.
33. Noel, (as above) 78 & 82.
34. *ibid,* 82 & 83; Duganne, *Twenty Months in the Department of the Gulf,* 141 & 142; Taylor, *Destruction & Reconstruction,* 141.
35. Duganne, *Twenty Months in the Department of the Gulf,* 143; Taylor, *Destruction & Reconstruction,* 141.
36. Noel, *A Campaign from Santa Fe to the Mississippi,* 82; OR, Vol. XXVI, Part 1, 223.

37. OR, Vol. XXVI, Part 1, 225; Taylor, *Destruction & Reconstruction,* 141.
38. Duganne, *Twenty Months in the Department of the Gulf,* 143 & 144; Noel, *A Campaign from Santa Fe to the Mississippi,* 82 & 83.
39. OR, Vol. XXVI, Part 1, 225.
40. Duganne, *Twenty Months in the Department of the Gulf,* 144 & 145.
41. *ibid,* 144, 145, 146, 147 & 148; OR, Vol. XXVI, Part 1, 224 & 225.
42. Irwin, *19th Army Corps,* 241.
43. OR, Vol. XXVI, Part 1, 224; Noel, *A Campaign from Santa Fe to the Mississippi,* 85.
44. Taylor, *Destruction & Reconstruction,* 141 & 142.
45. OR, Vol. XXVI, Part 1, 226; Taylor, *Destruction & Reconstruction,* 141 & 142.
46. OR, Vol. XXVI, Part 1, 217 & 218.
47. *ibid,* 219; Irwin, *19th Army Corps,* 242.
48. Duganne, *Twenty Months in the Department of the Gulf,* 157.
49. *ibid,* 158.
50. Noel, *Campaign from Santa Fe to the Mississippi,* 85.

INDEX